Written on the Flyleaf

A Christian Faith in the Light of Other Faiths

Peter D. Bishop

Written on the Flyleaf

A Christian Faith
in the Light of Other Faiths

EPWORTH PRESS

0 7162 0519 X

First published in Britain 1998
by Epworth Press
20 Ivatt Way
Peterborough PE3 7PG

Typeset by Regent Typesetting, London
and printed in Great Britain by
Biddles Ltd, Guildford and King's Lynn

Contents

Preface

Do religious believers live in ghettos? Many would assume
that they do, and the signs of narrowness and intolerance
required to support such an assumption are all too easy to
find among believers of all kinds. If you have a religious belief
it is probably easier to shut yourself off mentally from those
whose beliefs differ from your own; to regard your own
beliefs as normative, and other beliefs as inaccurate, misleading, or downright crazy. But to do that might be a bad
mistake. The great nineteenth-century pioneer scholar of
religions, Max Müller, said in a favourite aphorism, 'he who
knows one knows none'. If you never consider seriously the
teaching and claims of religions other than your own, you
cannot even understand your own properly. There's a
thought!

We live at a time when knowledge of other people's
religions, cultures and ideologies is increasingly accessible.
Travel and television bring the sights and sounds, the words
and wisdom of a variety of religions within the everyday
world of an increasing number of people. It is more and more
difficult to inhabit an enclosed religious world, and to ignore
the cries and the claims of religions and systems of thought
which are not our own. That need not be a threat. Indeed, if
our own religious traditions appear tired and unconvincing,
it may be that we can find refreshment for jaded palates in
re-examining our own faith traditions in the light of the
religions of other people.

That is what this book sets out to do. It is a personal

reflection, arising out of a curiously mixed career in which the work of a Methodist Minister (and for seven years, of a Presbyter of the Church of South India) has been intertwined with the study and teaching of Indian religions. Over a period of thirty-five years both activities have been pursued, with an almost equal division between times when one or the other has been the full-time job. Looking back on my own personal development, I recognize how great has been the influence of Indian thought upon my own religious beliefs and spiritual life. Almost everything I now think and believe has written alongside it in the margins and between the lines some element of the insights of other faiths. Inevitably, that results in a critical set of attitudes towards one's own faith. But on the whole the result, I believe, is positive. This book sets out to explore spirituality, belief, the proper limits of self-interest, ethics, and the journey of faith in the light of other faiths. The conclusion is that as we make progress in our religious quest we may find ourselves, to our surprise, exploring new scenery, crossing cultural boundaries, and as a result waking up to new ways of believing and practising our faith.

Many people have helped to form the ideas which lie behind this book, and among them have been my own teachers, colleagues and students. I am grateful to them all. An earlier and longer draft of the book included much more on the New Testament than it now does, and I was grateful at that stage to Professor Kenneth Grayston for his perceptive comments and corrections, some of which influence what has survived from that draft. Once again, I am grateful to Sarah Ball for unstinting help and advice throughout a long period of gestation.

Peter D. Bishop

I

Written in Pencil on the Flyleaf

Behind what is written here there lies a personal religious quest, stretching back over thirty years and forming a puzzling weave made up of many different threads. On the one hand there is a personal religious commitment arising, as such things often do, out of personal experience rather than out of dispassionate intellectual enquiry. On the other hand, that commitment has had to bear the searching light of academic study and investigation not only of the history of Christianity but also of other major religious traditions. The study of other great world religions has so greatly enlarged and changed my understanding of religions as a whole that it has necessarily affected my interpretation of Christianity. It is with the contribution of the insights of other religions to an open-minded and liberal Christian faith that this book is concerned. The essential question that is being addressed in what follows is, can Christian faith be illumined and given fresh life by insights drawn from other religions?

It is inevitable that most people with a religious commitment nurture their beliefs and religious activities within systems that are largely closed and self-contained. We grow up in or come to accept a particular tradition, absorb its assumptions, share its ethos, and may be only marginally aware of alternatives. In spite of the growth of the ecumenical movement this century, and of the wider ecumenism that has increased knowledge of the world's religions, most practitioners of religion are likely to have at best a hazy view of other people's religions. So it was for me. My own initial contact, with British Methodism, was followed by a theology degree course that introduced me to some of the mysteries of New Testament Greek and Biblical Hebrew, to church history and theology, but which provided only a cursory look at other religions. It was a kind of double accident that introduced me to the study of a particular set of non-Christian traditions.

The first accident occurred when as a theological student I uttered, with what now appears to have been a foolhardy confidence in the judgment of others, that undoubtedly scriptural phrase, 'Here am I; send me'. Unlike Isaiah, whose famous statement resulted in his being sent to a people whose wits were dulled and eyes blinded, my rather less significant offer produced the suggestion that I should go to India. There, working for seven years in the Church of South India, I was to learn far more than I ever could have given, and to come into contact with Hindus whose wits were sharp and whose spirituality was undoubtedly genuine and probably profound.

The second accident occurred as part of the preparation for India. I was permitted by the church to enrol in a Master's degree course in what the University of Manchester archaically called 'Comparative Religion'. That period of study was for me so full of the excitement of new ideas as to bear almost the marks of revelation. To attempt seriously to study a part of the great traditions of India was the first stage in a long process of re-adjustment in which everything that had previously been learned and assumed would be challenged. At the time I was only vaguely aware of the possible implications of such study. But I arrived in India, in 1964, already conscious of the importance of trying to understand the Hindu world, and with a sense that to do that might be more important for me than to attempt to convert Hindus to Christianity. Experience in India was to confirm that initial impression.

After a short and uncomfortable stay in Madras, in which

English-speaking city I was placed to begin the tortuous process of trying to learn Tamil, I was fortunate enough to be sent, with my wife, small son and baby daughter, to Vellore. Vellore was in most respects a fairly ordinary and medium-sized south Indian town, a district headquarters with law courts, a busy bazaar, and a remarkably well-preserved thirteenth-century fort inside which we were to live. But in one respect Vellore was extraordinary. As one drove into the town along the dusty road from the east, there appeared a great complex of buildings, many of them several storeys high, which provided a startling contrast to the small houses and shops lining the other side of the road. That was the site of the Christian Medical College Hospital, one of the leading teaching hospitals of India and a centre of medical excellence that would bear comparison with some of the best hospitals of Europe or the USA. CMC Hospital had been founded at the beginning of the century by an American woman missionary of exceptional talent and enthusiasm who fulfilled in a remarkable fashion her ambition to provide first nursing and then medical care of women by women in an area where the customs in the late nineteenth and early twentieth centuries ordained that women could not be attended by male doctors. Dr Ida Scudder's work had begun in one room in 1900, and that was followed only two years later by the building of a forty-bed hospital. In 1909 Ida Scudder fulfilled part of her ambition by opening a School of Nursing; in 1918 a medical school for women, training licentiates in medicine, came into being. In 1924 the hospital moved to a larger site to enable expansion, and today that has grown into a well-equipped and up-to-date 1500 bed hospital. The women's medical school became a fully-fledged Medical College in 1942, and five years later, in changing circumstances, men were admitted to train alongside the women.

When we arrived in Vellore Ida Scudder had recently died; the hospital and medical college which were her remarkable memorials dominated the town. Within and around the hospital and college (situated in the countryside four miles outside the town) there had grown up a cosmopolitan community of medical and para-medical workers drawn from all over India and from many parts of the world. Most of the medical and nursing staff in Vellore were Christians, and they saw their work in Vellore (often rewarded at a fraction of the salaries that highly skilled people could have earned elsewhere) as a fulfilment of their Christian vocation. On Sunday mornings many of those people – mostly Indians from different language areas of the country, but also with a sprinkling of Americans, Swiss, Australians, English, Scots; students and staff and families – crowded into St John's Church for Christian worship. At the end of our first year in India I was appointed Presbyter of St John's, and so became the minister of one of the most remarkable Christian congregations to be found anywhere.

My study of Hinduism, and also of Tamil and then Sanskrit, continued alongside the work at St John's and other activities of the Madras Diocese of the Church of South India. Trying to learn the language brought me into contact with two different kinds of south Indians: my last Tamil teacher was a great enthusiast for the revival of Tamil culture and language then sweeping the area, and inevitably a supporter of the Tamil nationalist party which came to power in Tamilnadu ('the country of the Tamils', formerly Madras State) in 1967; my Sanskrit teacher was an elderly *brahmin* lawyer living through a period in which previous *brahmin* dominance was being broken in south India and political control taken from them. Both were men of great humanity and integrity, and fine examples of their different Hindu cultures.

Although 'dialogue' was not the fashionable word it was to become later, it occurred to me that it might be good to try to establish a regular meeting between members of the local Hindu communities and members of St John's Church. I wrote a letter to about one hundred and forty Hindus in the

town, inviting them to a series of meetings in the church hall
of St John's, and encouraged the St John's people to attend.
The idea was to meet once a fortnight to discuss some central
piece of teaching in Hinduism or Christianity, and in a subsequent meeting to consider the teaching on a similar subject
in the other religion (for example, concepts of God or the
divine in the two religions). The meetings were not a complete success. Very few members of St John's congregation
came to them. Of course, they were busy people, and had
many other concerns. But I suspect that there was also a feeling that there was something unnecessary or improper about
Christians gathering to discuss matters of faith with members
of other religious communities; that what Christians should
be doing is proclaiming the Christian gospel, not exposing
themselves to the claims of other faiths. A rather different
reservation about one paragraph in my letter of invitation
was raised by my diocesan bishop, Dr Lesslie Newbigin, a
man of quite extraordinary ability and a model of what a
Christian minister and bishop could be. The offending words
in my invitation to local Hindus were:

> We should like to make it clear that the intention in calling
> these meetings is not that of seeking the conversion of non-
> Christians to the Christian faith. We rather seek to under-
> stand the other great religions of India and – if it be
> possible – to help others, and ourselves, to understand the
> contribution that Christianity might make to the whole life
> of society.

Lesslie Newbigin wrote:

> . . . I am not happy about the language of the paragraph
> beginning, 'We should like to make it clear . . .' I under-
> stand and accept the basic intention of the paragraph but
> think that as it stands it is not defensible. If one accepts the
> view that religion is concerned with what ultimately and

finally matters to us, I don't think this kind of language is possible. A merely academic discussion on religious questions is futile. I would quote the remark of a Marxist in Prague who said: 'The only kind of Christian I am interested in talking to is the one who wants to convert me.' If the Christianity about which we are talking is not concerned to convert men to Christ, then it is not the genuine article. Nor is religion rightly understood in terms of its contribution to society. Having spent four years in intensely intimate dialogue with Hindus in the Ramakrishna Ashram at Conjeevaram, I was deeply impressed with the difference between the two approaches to the matter. There were always some who came merely for academic discussion of the religion but there were one or two who were as deeply concerned to convert me to the Hindu position as I was concerned to convert them to the Christian. It was with these that really deep dialogue and really deep friendship developed.[1]

From my copies of this correspondence I see that I wrote a vigorous, perhaps even brash, rejoinder. Thirty years later one of the things I recognize in my letter is the unassailable confidence of (comparative) youth. The bishop, much busier than I, allowed the matter to rest there, and no doubt demonstrated his wisdom in allowing a young presbyter to make his own experiments. Some of the points I made in reply, however, seem to me still to be valid, and worth mentioning because they indicate something of what I thought – and still think – underlies dialogue. First, I objected to the criticism of 'a merely academic discussion'.

Does a discussion really suffer if it is undertaken in an academic way? Surely the use of academic discipline and methods is a help rather than a hindrance to genuine understanding. An academic discussion is to be valued and sought precisely because it seeks to be objective and because its aim is the truth. I see little prospect for a discussion between entrenched opponents belabouring one another with their presuppositions. The great problem of religious dialogue, as I see it, is that participants (especially if they are Christian) are prevented from genuinely considering the claims of other faiths because they cannot get away from their own presuppositions and put themselves, however tentatively, in the other man's place.

That is a significant charge to make against Christians. Of course, it could equally well be made against members of other faith-communities. Religions claim to provide access to ideas and experiences which are an important part of human understanding. They purport to mediate truths about the human condition and human destiny.

Yet it is necessary to recognize that religion has to do with questions of belief and the choice of commitment. There is no absolute or empirical way in which religious faith can be proved to be true, in a modern scientific sense. Indeed, that is partly why the word 'faith' is appropriate. It involves a commitment to what cannot be rationally or scientifically proved; the acceptance of a way of life and a set of values that the believer dares to accept, not in spite of the evidence – such faith would simply be foolishness – but in the absence of absolute incontrovertible evidence. That is what the author of the Letter to the Hebrews seemed to suggest when he described faith as what gives 'substance to our hopes and convinces us of realities we cannot see', or to translate more literally, that faith is what 'convinces us of the pragmatic value of what we cannot see' (*pragmaton elegchos ou blepomenon*).[2] Adherents of different faiths coming to dialogue are never in a position to say, 'as a matter of fact, my religion is true and yours is false'. The tendency to make such claims is a major cause both of misunderstanding and of bigotry.

Dialogue between people of different faiths is necessarily between those whose commitments are different, but must also be between those who are willing to set aside the desire simply to state their faith as though it were incontrovertible fact. There is no need to water down one's faith in order to engage in dialogue; but there is no possibility of people who confuse religious faith with verifiable scientific knowledge engaging in dialogue. They are likely to be perplexed and offended by the other's inability to accept 'the facts', but not to have the gift of listening to what the partner in dialogue says. A Christian fundamentalist in dialogue with an ayatollah might make an amusing sight, but it is unlikely to be instructive or to enlarge anyone's faith. An academic objectivity is one tool by which dialogue might be made fruitful, by encouraging participants to learn and to understand what the other person is actually saying. A modern Buddhist writer, H. Saddhatissa, commenting on the Buddhist principle of 'Right Speech', has said that much conversation consists of 'a series of interrupted monologues'.[3] The danger of dialogue between those who do not recognize the true nature of the faiths of those involved is that it is likely to become just such a series of interrupted monologues. Academic objectivity can help overcome that problem by encouraging the art of listening to what the other person is saying, and by making the attempt to put oneself in the other person's place.

I agree with Lesslie Newbigin that dialogue is likely to be most profitable between people who are serious about their respective faiths and committed to them. But that does not mean that dialogue must proceed on the assumption that its aim is to convert. Dialogue may be intended to deepen our understanding of other people's faith. But a dialogue that begins with the assumption that conversion ought to take place is surely corrupted from the beginning. Conversion should not be the aim, although it will always be a risk of dialogue. To engage in genuine discussion with people of other faiths is for all participants to risk change: to risk changing one's own perceptions of other faiths; and to risk a change in the understanding of one's own faith. There is a kind of conversion that is not from one faith to another, nor the stark *metanoia* or turning around of the New Testament, but a continual process of 'conversion', in which our understanding and practice of faith constantly develops and changes as part of the process of growth. It is in dialogue that people make themselves especially vulnerable to that kind of conversion. And it requires a combination of a willingness to declare one's own faith, but also to acknowledge that the consequences of any act of dialogue for any of the participants are in the hands of God. William Johnston put it very well in a letter to a fellow Catholic who wondered whether in dialogue there is a danger of abandoning the gospel. Johnston wrote:

> In dialogue we preach the entire Gospel because we love the Gospel and want to share its treasures with people we love. We put no pressure on anyone to accept it. No beguiling promises. No stern threats. No charming enticements. No malicious bribes. No backstairs politics. . . . And so it is entirely up to those who hear our word. They accept what they want; they leave what they don't want. We never break into the inner sanctum of conscience where the human person is alone with God.[4]

Such was the basis of that series of meetings in Vellore. A group of intelligent, well-educated Hindus, many of them lawyers in Vellore, began to meet with me fortnightly over a period of two or three years. Some of them had been educated in Christian schools and colleges, and knew the Bible better than many Western Christians would have done. Many surprised me with their knowledge of English literature and poetry. Of course, they also knew their own traditions – some were *advaitists*, some *visishtadvaitists* – and the

Sanskrit and Tamil texts.[5] We had long discussions, in which they disagreed with one another as well as with me, and between which I constantly had to go back to both Christian and Hindu sources to try to keep up with them. They seemed inordinately impressed by the fact that I was having lessons in Sanskrit, and so taking pains to try to understand Hindu traditions. That proved to be the opening of a door, and an important first lesson in dialogue.

But whatever they thought of me, I was greatly impressed by them. They were deeply serious about their own traditions and firmly committed to them. Their exposition of those traditions was often sophisticated and subtle, but they were firm believers in the essential doctrines which lay behind their sometimes abstruse discussions. They were also personally impressive. They struck me as people of great honesty and compassion, and of genuine spirituality. I became convinced that their traditions could produce men (and no doubt also women) of God. That was something to reflect on when I thought about a Christian theology of mission.

But more important, so far as the subject of this book is concerned, was the way in which this encounter with a group of devout and learned Hindus began to enhance my understanding of my own Christian faith. Among the subjects in which such influences could be felt were prayer and meditation. I began to think about Indian systems of yoga, and how they might be used in a Christian rather than a Hindu context to encourage meditation and contemplation. Later, I was to read some of Patanjali's *Yoga Sutras* and make some attempt to articulate ways in which Christians, without any threat to their own beliefs, could use techniques of yoga to help their own prayer.[6]

The period was the 1960s, the decade of *Honest to God* and the popularizing of Tillich and Bonhoeffer which occurred in that book and in other publications. Dialogue helped to enlarge my own understanding of what that aweful, tantalizing and much misunderstood word 'God' might mean. Looking back now at a slim volume of sermons published around the time I left India, I can see that those ideas were not a matter of 'merely academic discussion' but a stimulus to Christian preaching and to the exposition of Christian faith in the demanding environment of St John's, Vellore.[7] I began to question one aspect of popular Christian devotion which seemed in any case to contradict orthodox Christian theology in a way I had not appreciated fully. That is, the association, particularly in hymns and prayers and popular devotion, of the words 'Jesus' and 'God'. Clearly, Christians have commonly believed that in Jesus Christ God revealed himself in a special way. But in orthodox theological terms that has not led to the conclusion that Jesus of Nazareth is to be identified completely with God. Christian teaching has said: if you want to know what God is like, look at Jesus. It is not possible to find everything there is to know about God by looking at Jesus, for God is too vast and mysterious for that; but it is possible to know a number of essential things about God through the 'window' that Jesus provides into God's nature. One can know, for example, that God is love; that he cares for every individual man and woman; that somehow God shares in the sufferings of the world; and that in the end he redeems that suffering and transforms it, just as Jesus transformed the suffering which ended his earthly life. That, I take it, is the orthodox Christian position, and it is expressed by those Christians who are careful about their terminology by distinguishing among other things between 'Jesus' (of Nazareth) and 'Christ' (the cosmic Christ), and of course between 'Jesus' and 'God'. But in popular usage many Christians have slid imperceptibly into the idea that 'Jesus' and 'God' are interchangeable terms, and so something of the profundity of the idea of God has been lost. God has too often been regarded as a special kind of man who could work miracles and solve problems. For many Hindus, the idea of identifying God with a person limited by space and time is absurd. And even great

Gods, like *Vishnu* and *Shiva*, are often regarded as simply vehicles or representations of the ineffable, absolute reality that is called *Brahman*. I began to see how inadequate concepts formed in fairly narrow Protestant contexts could be enlarged and enriched by discussion with Hindus.

In a number of ways, some of which I shall discuss in later chapters, my Christian understanding was changed by that series of fascinating encounters: changed, but not I think diluted and certainly not destroyed. Indeed, Christianity became more credible when reinterpreted in the light of other faiths.

My own tentative experiment with dialogue was in no sense a pioneering effort. Many much more distinguished people had been engaged in the process, and it seemed that real pioneering work, at great depth, had been done by a number of Catholics. One of the great figures in Christian-Hindu dialogue in India was Bede Griffiths, and on a number of occasions he visited Vellore and I was able to meet him. Bede Griffiths was one of the most truly remarkable people in modern religious history. The story of his early life has been told in the beautifully written autobiography, *The Golden String*. There he told of his student life at Oxford and his conversion to Christian faith just a little after the conversion of his much better-known tutor C. S. Lewis, with whom he established a life-long friendship; of an experiment in communal living in the Cotswolds where an attempt – full of contradictions – to avoid the worst evils of the modern industrial world led to a life of extraordinary frugality; of his resolve to become a monk, and his entry into the Benedictine Order. It was in the late 1950s that Bede Griffiths left England for India, where eventually he settled in a small ashram in Kulittalai, near Tiruchirapalli in south India. The ashram was a place of great simplicity, consisting of a few thatched buildings, with mud floors, and a chapel which was partly open-air and offered the rare sight of a covering over the altar decorated with Sanskrit slokas, or verses, from

Indian scriptures. Father Griffiths lived there for many years in the style of a Hindu *sannyasi*, dressing in an orange robe, eating very simple vegetarian food, praying, meditating, and talking to those who visited or stayed at the ashram about religion, spirituality, and Christian-Hindu dialogue. Few Europeans succeeded in adapting as he did to the simplicity and self-denial of such a life, and it undoubtedly encouraged Hindus to regard him as a genuinely holy man. My own respect and admiration for Bede Griffiths was very great. His gentle nature, deep sincerity, and considerable intellectual gifts marked him out as a rare and fine example of a particularly demanding style of Christian living and of inter-religious encounter.[8] Father Griffiths enhanced my own understanding of the value of dialogue. Those who have read such books as *Return to the Centre* and *The Marriage of East and West* will know of the nature of his adventurous attempts to combine Catholic theology and spirituality with the insights gained from his long and arduous exploration of Hindu religion and culture. For me, one of the lessons learned from him was that the religious traditions of the East can encourage the development of some of the finest aspects of Christian character, not least by emphasizing the importance of restraining excesses of egotism and self-indulgence and by looking beyond the surface to the depths of human nature and experience. To switch mentally from a picture of Bede Griffiths at Kulittalai to the egotistical posturing of some Western clerics is to be shocked into a recognition of how much Christians could benefit from a greater knowledge of the best of Eastern religious traditions.

Bede Griffiths' extensive knowledge of Hindu traditions was a help to me in another piece of work I undertook during my second tour in India. During a furlough in Britain in 1968 I had enrolled as an external student at King's College, London, for a PhD, and on returning to India I began to gather material. The subject was the interaction between two great figures of modern Hinduism, Swami

Vivekananda and Sri Aurobindo, and Western influences.[9] Issues that relate to dialogue were involved to some extent in the research. Swami Vivekananda was the first person who could be described accurately as a Hindu missionary to the West. His appearance at the World Parliament of Religions at Chicago in 1893 had a startling effect upon a much wider audience who read his speeches in the newspapers. Vivekananda presented a vigorous criticism of Christian missionaries, claiming that they dismissed as heathen nonsense what they did not understand,[10] and asserting that Hinduism was not simply the equal of Christianity but in many respects its superior. Swami Vivekananda later founded the Ramakrishna Mission (in 1897), and established a 'Foreign Branch' which had some success in promoting forms of Hinduism (especially *advaita*) and in making converts in the USA and Europe.

Sri Aurobindo, like Vivekananda, a Bengali, had a very different history and a different set of reactions to Western influences. He had been sent to England at the age of seven by his father, who wanted him to have an entirely English education and who actually forbade any contact with Indians whilst in England. Aurobindo received private tuition and schooling in England, and then proceeded to Cambridge, where the embargo on Indian contacts was inevitably broken. He joined a radical Indian student society, dedicated to India's freedom, and returned to India in 1893 to become a leading figure in the nationalist movement in Bengal in the turbulent political climate there between 1905 and 1910. Two periods in prison led Aurobindo to reflect further on India's culture and religion and their relationship to nationalism, and in 1910 he fled from Bengal to the French territory of Pondicherry. In that south Indian town on the Coromandel coast he eventually established a substantial and unusual ashram, wrote extensively, and constructed an original system of philosophy in his 'integral yoga', which employed Western as well as Indian concepts.

Bede Griffiths had been interested for a long time in Aurobindo's complex and difficult writings, and was particularly impressed by possible parallels between aspects of Aurobindo's thought and Christian theology. He wrote:

> His (Aurobindo's) system is already half-way I would say towards Christianity. The whole idea of the evolution of matter through man to the divine and the descent of the Supermind to raise man to the divine life seems to me to fit perfectly with the theology of St Paul. Christ is the point where the upward movement of the divine life, and the new humanity emerges with the descent of the Spirit at Pentecost.[11]

Bede Griffiths was kind enough to read the whole of the draft of my thesis and to engage in helpful discussion and correspondence about some of the issues.

The research itself gave further help to my appreciation of some of the many varieties of Hindu thought and practice, and enhanced my understanding of the often subtle interaction between the great religious systems and cultures of the East and Western thought. That, too, had an inevitable impact upon the ways in which I was to understand and interpret Christian life and teaching.

Most of my time in India, of course, had been spent in concerns other than dialogue. In addition to a theoretically full-time job organizing and writing correspondence courses which the diocese of Madras provided for Hindus and Muslims who wanted to know something about Christianity and the New Testament, there was St John's Church with its demanding diet of Sunday worship and preaching. St John's also had a daughter church in the small but beautiful Indian-style chapel of St Luke's at the leprosy hospital at Karigiri, situated in an isolated area some ten miles from Vellore. The care of leprosy patients has long been a concern of the church in India, as elsewhere, and at Karigiri patients from a wide surrounding area, where leprosy was endemic, were treated. Drugs could control the disease, and could do so especially effectively when it was caught in the early stages; surgery could correct hands and feet deformed by the disease; and precautions against damaging limbs in which sensation may have been deadened could be taken by wearing Karigiri-made chappals. The hospital staff were also engaged constantly in research, especially in attempts to find ways of preventing the disease rather than just curing it.

Most of the patients were villagers from the local area, and so Sundays at St Luke's included the stern test of trying to deliver (mercifully short and simple) sermons in Tamil. I can still remember the enormously lengthy process of trying to write such sermons, taking drafts to my Tamil teacher, finding that there were concepts that simply would not translate, and having the interesting and valuable experience of submitting to a critique of a sermon from a Hindu. The Tamil teacher, as an enthusiastic follower of the Tamil nationalist party, the DMK,[12] also wanted me to conclude sermons with the oratorical flourishes which were common among DMK politicians, whose perorations often contained such phrases as 'long live Tamilnadu', 'long live the DMK'. The concession to the different nature of the sermon was the suggestion that substitutes such as 'long live Jesus Christ' could be made, and such was his enthusiasm for this that I sometimes felt compelled to write down the theologically curious words, only to ignore them when it came to delivering the message. At Karigiri there was a divide between patients and staff. Many of the senior medical staff were not Tamils, and so wanted a sermon in English. The struggle to read an extremely limited sermon in Tamil at a level thought to be suitable for Hindu villagers, and then to say something on the same subject but at quite a different level and in English was one I engaged in, but never I think with any real success. What it did for the congregation I did not know; certainly, it often confused me.

There was another aspect to those Sunday morning services that struck me when I began to visit Karigiri. That was the enthusiastic way in which the leprosy patients, mostly very poor, usually Hindus, often disfigured or crippled by one of the most feared diseases in India, would sing the Tamil Christian lyrics, and the intense way in which they engaged in responses to prayers and attended to the service. The surprise was two-fold. One was that adherents of one religion would so happily pray and sing in the vocabulary of another. The other was that people who suffered so greatly could still show such courage and hope and faith.

But there is another aspect of dialogue, often overlooked by those whose discussions are entirely intellectual, which was brought out by the experience of Karigiri. There has been a long process of dialogue in many parts of the world expressed not in words but in actions and service. Examples of co-operation and mutual help in these areas can be found between Muslims and Hindus, Jews and Christians, and many other groups often thought of as antagonistic to one another. And practical co-operation may be a more effective way of cultivating understanding between members of different religious communities than discussion and debate. Examples of such co-operation and mutual caring can also help to break down the stereotypes that are still often found in writings about religions: the assumptions, for example, that Sikhs are aggressive, Hindus are tolerant, and Christians are dogmatic and intolerant. Examples can be found to justify all these assertions; but as with most grand generalizations, they can be grossly misleading. One example of such stereotyping is found in frequent parodies, especially in Western writing, of Christian mission. Some of those parodies can be justified quite easily. Some Christian missionaries have been remarkably insensitive and blindly dogmatic, intent only on converting 'the heathen' to their own narrow ways. But for many of the Christians I knew in India, whether Indian or Western, mission was expressed through service more than by words, and expressed what for them was a great desire to demonstrate their belief in a God of love through humanitarian service. The needs of the poor, the afflicted and the oppressed could bring together Hindus, Christians, Muslims and others with no sense of incongruity or conflict. When, much later, I wrote about the interaction between the ideas and practices of non-violent resistance in Mahatma Gandhi and Martin Luther King Jr, I partly had in mind the kind of dialogue between people in different religious and cultural traditions which results not in theoretical statements of belief but in practical courses of action.[13] Karigiri was one example of common need and practical service leading to deeper inter-religious understanding.

Thinking about the influence of other religions on an understanding of Christian faith did not stop when I returned to Britain in 1971. After the inevitable culture shock of returning to the West and the feeling of passing through a time warp in moving from a united church to denominationally divided Britain, I was transmuted from Church of South India presbyter to Methodist minister, but managed to continue the work on Vivekananda and Aurobindo. Then, in 1975, I moved to the then Brighton Polytechnic to lecture, in a Humanities Department, in the history of religions and especially in Indian religions.[14] Gradually there developed parallel courses in what could have been (but are not) described as 'Indian influences in the West' – that is, courses related to the communities of Muslims, Sikhs and Hindus in Britain whose origins lie in the Indian sub-continent, and in some cases in East Africa. Relationships between people of different religions in Britain had come to be bound up with wider issues which included race relations, public policy and education. Inter-disciplinary courses were developed which dealt with questions arising in multi-cultural Britain in a number of ways. Inevitably, religious belief and practice among British Asians was one of the subjects which remained

central to the courses with which I was particularly concerned, in addition to courses that had to do with Hinduism
in its Indian context. The study of religions within courses
of this kind became a matter of much more than religious
interest alone. In modern Britain a sympathetic knowledge of
a variety of religious traditions has become a necessary tool
for the development of good race relations and the cultivation of an open and tolerant multi-cultural society, in addition to the intrinsic interest of religious ideas and practices.

It soon became apparent that there was a profound
difference between talking about and teaching religion in
Britain and doing so in an Indian context. In India there
remains a climate of opinion in which religion is taken with
great seriousness, and people expect that religion, of whatever kind, will play a part in their neighbours' lives. For the
most part it is taken for granted that everyone will have a
religion of one kind or another, although differences between
religion as belief and religion as culture must be allowed for
in that recognition. Mainland Britain, on the other hand, has
become an extremely 'secular' part of the world, where
religion is regarded by large numbers of people as irrelevant
at best or foolish or mistaken at worst. What it is that constitutes 'secularization' is a matter of debate; but there can be
no doubt that modern Britain, in common with some other
areas of Western Europe, has become generally inhospitable
to organized religion. When Dietrich Bonhoeffer wrote from
his prison cell in Nazi Germany about how one might be able
to live as a Christian in a 'world come of age' – that is, a
world in which there appears to be no need for supernatural
explanations or resources – he was pointing to one of the
great issues for late twentieth-century Christianity and
raising questions that remain largely unanswered.

The scale of secularism in Britain might also be thought to
reflect changing attitudes between the generations. Certainly,
many Christian congregations contain considerably more
over-fifties than under twenty-fives. And the pattern is not

restricted to Christian churches. One feature of life in British Asian and Jewish communities is a concern about young people, and how secular attitudes in the world around them may detach them from the religious practices and cultural values of their elders. The student world, therefore, particularly reflects the influence of secular patterns of thought.

It may be because of the historical background and civic role of Christianity in British life that it is Christian faith and practice that is affected most by this strongly flowing sea of secular thought. A more tolerant attitude is often shown towards Eastern religions, perhaps because in a British context they reflect rather more the religious and cultural interests of disadvantaged minorities. However well-founded such explanations may be, it is certainly the case that it is easier to arouse and sustain sympathetic enquiry into non-Christian than Christian religion among secular undergraduates – a point that appears to have been missed by those politicians and churchmen who have campaigned for a stronger emphasis on Christian teaching in school curricula. Paradoxical as it may seem, when trying to cultivate an understanding of religion among students the teacher may be best advised to approach the subject via the lesser-known religions of the East rather than to clash head on with the prejudices about Christianity that abound and the inevitably negative aspects of a religion that is related historically to one's own society. Another advantage of an acquaintance with Eastern religions appears: the study of the traditions of the East can help people to appreciate more clearly what religion is, and how varied it is; to indicate how common it is for varied traditions and interpretations to exist side-by-side within a single religion; to demonstrate the significance of differences between popular and intellectual forms of religion; and possibly to illuminate one set of beliefs through an awareness of others. Although in my experience most students began to study religions from a strongly secular and often anti-religious perspective, most overcame their prejudices quickly and arrived at a position from which they were able to consider religious traditions and the life of the believer with a sympathetic attitude even though few were themselves likely to be believers in any religion.

So far I have been referring to Eastern, and particularly Indian, religion. But another necessary development at Brighton was the examination of other aspects of multi-cultural Britain than those concerning Muslims, Sikhs and Hindus. For example, an understanding of the problems British people have with newcomers could be helped if it were to be put into an historical context. We included in our courses an analysis of responses to nineteenth-century immigration, and found many remarkable similarities between the experience of, and British responses to, nineteenth-century Jewish and twentieth-century New Commonwealth immigrants.

The issue of relationships with Jewish people then raised another set of questions, the importance of which has been recognized increasingly in recent years. It was at Manchester that I first began to think about the significance of a Jewish understanding of Judaism for a better-informed reading of parts of the New Testament. The doyen of Comparative Religion at Manchester in those days was Professor S. G. F. Brandon, whose many publications included *Jesus and the Zealots* and *The Fall of Jerusalem and the Christian Church*. I had a high regard for Professor Brandon's scholarship, enjoyed his lectures, and read what I could of his writings. His controversial views of the significance of Judaism for the history of Christian beginnings stimulated my interest. But it was at Brighton that I began to read more recent works by both Jewish and Christian authors on the trial of Jesus and other matters that affected an interpretation of the New Testament. Increasingly, in the wake of the Second World War and the horrors of the Holocaust, scholars were looking afresh at those elements of Christian teaching that appear to have anti-Jewish connotations. An interest in questions of

Christian-Jewish relations became a small but significant addition to my own developing understanding of religion in general, and inevitably influenced my reading of the New Testament. A reading of Jewish history was reinforced by a visit to Israel. The salutary experience, for a European Christian, of walking around the Holocaust Museum in Jerusalem and the Museum of the Dispersion in Tel Aviv enhanced the feeling that Christians handling their own traditions must come to terms with the persistent anti-Jewishness of much of Christian Europe throughout most of its history. Participation in an international conference in 1988, commemorating the Holocaust, or *Shoah*, opened the doors to a whole flood of new information and ideas on the subject. It became clear that only the most sensitive and aware of Christian preachers could avoid anti-Jewish suggestions in their proclamations of Christian faith. That raises further questions about how a religion resting to some degree upon belief in a unique revelation can relate to other religions. The 'other faiths' with which this book is chiefly concerned are those of Hinduism and Buddhism, and yet the Christian history of the treatment of Judaism does show how strong the temptation has been for Christians to reject even so close a partner as Judaism in order to buttress its own claims to unique truth. Is that inevitable, or is there room for mutual enrichment? That my own answers to those questions are 'no' to the first and 'yes' to the second is no doubt obvious. Yet the relationship between Judaism and Christianity throws the question into particularly sharp focus.

All Christians, of whatever theological background or inclination, are likely to agree that some knowledge of the history and beliefs of the Jewish people is a necessary precondition for an understanding of the background to their own faith. The message of the New Testament is seen to relate closely to that of the Old Testament. Fundamental parts of the Hebrew Bible – creation, the word of God spoken through the prophets, the covenant, the holiness of God – are accepted as parts of a revelation taken up into the Christian revelation. The message of Jesus, it is agreed, must be seen against the background of his own religious traditions, of which he said, 'I did not come to abolish but to fulfil.' Indeed, as modern scholarship increasingly asserts, Jesus can only be understood in the light of a sympathetic acquaintance with his own religious and cultural context, that is with the various strands of Judaism in the first century.

Not many Christians have a problem with explorations of the Jewish background of Jesus, although there are real differences among Christians about how to read such evidence and apply it to their own faith. For many Christians and for far too long – and this is a common and understandable Jewish complaint – Judaism has been seen only as a form of pre-Christian religion, an Old Testament ending in the first century. Yet few Christians who think seriously about the matter would be willing to concede that the revelation which comes later must completely supersede what has gone before. Such a view would expose Christians themselves to far too dangerous a criticism from Islam, the last of the three great Semitic religions. Just as many Christians would wish for Muslims to assess Christian faith sympathetically and on its own terms, so they will see the need to deal in a similar way with Judaism.

An increasing number of Christians are able to take a more positive view of Judaism, agreeing that developments well after the first century, in the rabbinic traditions, in the Talmud, in the life of the synagogues, and in the experience of living as the covenant people in the diaspora have much to contribute to Christian self-understanding. A scholarly knowledge of Judaism both before and after the first century and an acquaintance with Jewish people today, can only deepen and enrich the understanding and use of the New Testament. There should be little disagreement on that point, whether Christians accept much of the recent Jewish critique of Christian beginnings, or whether they hold to a more traditional position.

After many challenging and interesting years at Brighton I made the impetuous decision to return finally to a church appointment, and spent three years in Bristol enjoying the company of different kinds of students as a chaplain, wrestling with the peculiarities of local church life, but also enjoying contact with many people of other faiths in the city. The Council of Christians and Jews was one forum in which regular meetings with Jews was both possible and rewarding. The Bristol Inter-Faith Group provided a much wider forum in which Muslims, Hindus, Sikhs, Jews, Buddhists, Christians, and others shared in celebrations, talked about their traditions, and practised a hospitality which was refreshingly wider than any one religious tradition could provide. The great nineteenth-century scholar, Max Müller, was surely right in his assertion that in terms of understanding religion, 'he who knows one knows none'. The refreshment of turning from the often introspective concerns of a small religious community to the wider interests and varied spiritual insights of the faiths found in a major British city was like turning from a scene of monochrome grey to gaze at a rainbow of colours. It was also the continuation of a long and delightful journey of discovery of the good things to be found in different faith communities, and a reinforcement of a desire to encourage a wider sympathy and greater tolerance between people of different faiths.

I had found that the minds of students could light up with interest and the stimulus of a new perspective when introduced to the great religions of India. I believe that many Westerners – including many Christians – are also ready for what has become worn and stale material to be lit up with new insights drawn from a set of different but complementary religious traditions. The following chapters are an invitation to join an exploration into ways in which familiar material can be shot through with new insights, and a tradition which for many has become tedious with repetition and misuse seen again with a new clarity.

T. S. Eliot, whose poetry and writing expressed in many ways the Anglican Christianity which he embraced in 1927, was also a man greatly indebted to the religious traditions of the East. His acquaintance with Indian religions was not that of a dilettante. As a graduate student at Harvard he studied Pali and Sanskrit, read portions of the *Vedas*, the *Upanishads* and the *Gita* in the original, and studied Patanjali's *Yoga Sutras* under the guidance of James Woods. He came to accept Christianity in a fairly traditional form and on its own grounds. Yet his writing continued to be enriched by all that he had learned from India. Cleo McNelly Kearns, in her study of Indian influences on T. S. Eliot, summarized his own appreciation of his mental journeys to the East in the following way:

As Eliot noted of his own exploration of the frontiers of philosophy and criticism, we may be 'enriched' by our travels across boundaries, but we cannot often convey very much of the material treasure back home. The wisdom we shall have acquired from such a journey will not be part of the argument that brings us to the conclusion; it will not be part of the book, but 'written in pencil on the flyleaf'.[15]

What follows here is not, so far as Christian faith is concerned, part of the argument that brings us to the conclusion. But as I have been immeasurably enriched by journeys across boundaries, so it is my hope that others will find in these pages a series of insights, written in pencil on the flyleaf in ways that will bring fresh understanding to familiar material.

2

Petitioners and Yogis

The casual observer attending some of the most popular kinds of Christian worship to be found today might be struck by the intensity and language of petitionary prayer. The New Testament exhortation to 'ask, and you will receive'[1] is likely to be taken very seriously, and God – or Jesus – will be asked to provide many things. There may also be a tendency to tell God all sorts of things which in more philosophical mood a worshipper might assume he already knows, and to do that in a language which is itself a badge of a special kind of piety. Prayers will be peppered with such phrases as 'Lord, we just want you to know . . .'. However fervent such prayer might be, it is unlikely to provide a spiritual diet on which a thoughtful worshipper can regularly feed.

On the other hand, the casual – and distant – observer of Buddhist and Hindu societies might assume that religions of the East have at their centre cross-legged yogis, sitting absorbed in concentration. Meditation is indeed an important part of Hindu and Buddhist practice. But it is far from being the only, or even the main, expression of prayer in those religions. Any actual acquaintance with Hindu and Buddhist practices on their home ground will make apparent the importance of petitionary prayer addressed to God or the gods, to *bodhisattvas* or even to gurus.[2] Popular worship at temples in India is replete with requests addressed to the temple deities, often for the most practical of things. Petitionary prayer is as common in the religions which arose in Asia as it is among Christians. Indeed, there is a remarkable similarity in styles of worship in the most popular traditions of many religions. One of the curious and mildly amusing features of the annual inter-faith celebration hosted by the Lord Mayor in Bristol was the number of items performed by different religious groups which included guitars, hand-clapping, and the singing of chorus-type songs. The all-singing, all-dancing, happy-clappy style of worship is not the prerogative of Christian evangelical groups. But then amidst the shallow noisiness would come a welcome period of silence, as a Buddhist group led a meditation on a particular theme, with a series of thoughts interrupted only by the tinkle of a small handbell.

Inter-faith celebrations of that kind are not only a way of satisfying curiosity about how other people do things, but also a reminder that mutual enrichment is possible between different faiths. Christianity has a rich tradition of spirituality, of meditation and contemplation, and of the teaching of great mystics. But little of that is allowed to penetrate popular Christian worship today. Such worship may be noisy and exuberant; it may be stolid and dull. But it almost certainly will be full of words and provide little opportunity for silent reflection. Of much current Christian worship it is possible to say: 'Well, that was an interesting piece of entertainment; but when was I supposed to worship? Where were the pools of quiet in which I could reflect?' Christians who feel the need for quiet reflection will probably have to take themselves off to a Quaker meeting in order to avail themselves of the opportunity. And even there, welcome as the quietness is, it is not easy to know what – other than one's personal thoughts – is meant to inform the use of silence. One can hardly turn to a neighbour at the end of an hour of silent worship in a Friends' Meeting and ask, 'How was that for you, then?'[3]

In spite of common features between faiths and their forms of worship there does seem to be a lack of teaching about meditation in Christian circles, and too great a willingness to accept crude petitionary prayer as staple fare in a Christian spiritual diet. The bald stereotype of Western activism and Eastern mysticism may be far too simplistic; but there are things to be learned from the religious traditions of the East which can greatly enhance Christian prayer and worship. Some of the earliest Western converts to forms of Hinduism and Buddhism were people who had become deeply dissatisfied with what they saw as the undue emphasis upon simple-minded petition among Christians. One of the commonest criticisms of Christianity made by converts to the *advaita vedanta* of the Ramakrishna Mission was that it did not provide adequate teaching about prayer and meditation. Gerald Heard expressed a widespread view among such converts when he wrote that:

> Christianity's one praxis [is] simple petitionary prayer. . . In the Vedanta meditation and contemplation are basic, and make a complete working psychology, while with this scientific knowledge there is, as a modern would expect and demand, a clear realization of the body-mind relationship. And all this rests, not on blind authority, but upon empirical work which any enquirer may repeat (indeed must repeat) and confirm for himself.[4]

That comparison may appear to be too shallow, and the suggestion that 'the one praxis' of Christianity is petitionary prayer absurd to anyone who knows anything about the rich traditions of Christian spirituality and mysticism. But it does reflect the kind of view which might still be gleaned from the observation of much Christian worship. An observer might be fortunate enough to chance upon churches in which the worship stimulates the spirit and preaching enlivens the mind, with perhaps even an opportunity for quiet prayer and reflection. But that could not be guaranteed. Indeed, such places can be found only with great difficulty. And it would be unusual to stumble across a church in which there is reflection upon the teachings and practices of the mystics. The practice of spirituality is not much taught in Christian churches, although it is central to the activities of some of the present-day alternatives to Christianity. Student experience in Brighton and the Inter-Faith Group in Bristol suggested that a large part of the appeal of Buddhist centres in Britain is that they offer guidance and practice in meditation, and that the pursuit of a developing spiritual practice is at the heart of their activities. By contrast, many Christian churches are associated in the public mind with an undue emphasis upon churchgoing as an end in itself, and with a constant preoccupation with maintaining the fabric and membership of the churches almost for their own sakes. Of course, such things are necessary, but they are central neither to religious nor to moral activity.

Is it possible that the well-tried methods of meditation and spiritual discipline that are found among Hindu and Buddhist traditions could inform and enliven Christian practice? And that in the process the trite prayers of the petitioners be rendered less inhospitable to serious reflection by an encounter with the yogis? The two are in any case not quite as separate as might appear. In Indian and Eastern religious traditions, as has been mentioned, lively and colourful worship and pious requests addressed to the deities co-exist with carefully constructed systems of meditation. The yogi always does his stuff surrounded, as it were, by crowds of more exuberant if less thoughtful worshippers. So too among Christians the traditions are not all to do with telling the Lord what he or she will know already, and asking so that the petitioner will receive. There are also the systems of mystical theology and of methods of meditation which were developed especially in the monastic traditions of Christianity but which spread much more widely. The Rule of St Benedict, the spiritual exercises of Ignatius Loyola, the writings of St Teresa and St John of the Cross are alive and in regular use. In some respects the influence of systems of meditation originally developed in the monasteries has grown as the ecumenical movement has encouraged Christians of many different traditions to appreciate and use that part of their heritage. Classes in meditation and practical advice about it can be found within Christian churches, although such things remain very much a minority interest among modern Christians. William Johnston wrote in his inimitable style and with reference to monks and nuns in his own Catholic tradition:

> Here are people whose lives are geared to *satori* (enlightenment), yet they feel that all is meaningless unless they are moving around the place making a noise in the name of Christian charity. If young people look to Hinduism and Buddhism for the contemplative education that they instinctively long for, may this not be because modern Christianity has projected the image of a churchgoing religion rather than a mystical one? May it not have too much bingo and too little mysticism?[5]

Teaching people to pray, or at least to meditate and reflect, is one of the principle duties of any religious movement; such teaching may have powerful secular as well as religious consequences. The art of being silent, of knowing when to listen as well as when to speak, of valuing quiet concentration as much as the noise of words, these are all qualities to be cherished. All should be inculcated by any religious community worth its salt.

What, then, is to be found in other traditions that might stimulate and guide practices of meditation and contemplation among Christians? Indian traditions tell us that we need to be comfortable, to calm our thoughts with slow and regular breathing, and to focus our wandering minds on a single point. The most popular of Hindu scriptures, the *Bhagavad Gita*, contains advice for this kind of basic beginning to prayer and meditation:

Having settled himself in a firm spot, with his own seat, not too high and not too low, and (having spread) a cloth, a skin and a kusa-grass over it; being seated, he should concentrate [literally 'make one-pointed'] the mind, controlling both the mind and the senses. Let him practise yoga, for the perfection of the self.[6]

The *Bhagavad Gita* (the name means 'The Song of the Lord') is the most popular of all Hindu scriptures, and so probably the most important in terms of the affect it has on Hindu life today. Some describe it as 'The New Testament of India'. My own Sanskrit teacher in India would insist that we read the *Bhagavad Gita* together, and his own early immersion in the text was demonstrated by the ease with which he could remember it. Once he had picked up a verse, he would close his eyes, rock gently backwards and forwards in his chair, and recite from memory the Sanskrit text of the *Gita*, seemingly with no limit to his power to recall as much of the text as might be required. It was the *Gita* that was burned into his memory. The *Gita* contains important teaching on *dharma*, or duty; on *samkhya* philosophy; and on the three paths to liberation, or salvation, which are the way of knowledge (especially of the sacred texts) and meditation, known as *jnana*; the way of action, including social and political action as well as the performance of ritual, known as *karma*; and the way of loving devotion to God, known as *bhakti*. In the course of all that, the *Gita* contains direct and practical teaching on meditation in a way that the Bible does not.

So in the verses quoted above the *Gita* tells us that in order to concentrate we have to be free of distractions of all kinds, including the overwhelming distraction of physical discomfort. The mind can only be controlled when the body is controlled. Having discovered how to sit, the meditator needs to relax, to breathe slowly and regularly; to focus attention, perhaps, on a picture (not too fussy), a flower, a candle, a tree – whatever helps to prevent the mind wandering away.

Meditation is also a form of relaxation (although it can be much more than that). And having become comfortable, we should encourage the stilling of a restless mind by fixing attention on a particular point – a symbol, or a familiar verse. 'That', wrote Bede Griffiths, 'is one of the key words in the understanding of meditation . . . concentration on a point.'[7]

The *Gita* provides detailed advice about what may be required to forget the claims and cries of the body in order to concentrate the mind. It advises that the head, neck and spine should all be kept in as straight a line as possible (6. 13). Concentration, it says, can be aided by 'not eating too little or too much; not sleeping too little or too much, but being in harmony' (6. 16). The harmony advocated here is reminiscent of the Buddha's Middle Way, a compromise between excessive self-denial and self-indulgence. The advice of the *Gita* is that one must try to relax, aided by regular, calm breathing, and that then concentration and meditation will follow. In its own particular language, the *Gita* is suggesting simple techniques which may be adopted by anyone who wants to meditate, whatever their religious beliefs and presuppositions. And for the Christian to take note of that advice is not to enter into an entirely alien world. For in the *Gita* there is also the belief that the strenuous discipline of serious prayer and meditation is not an end in itself, but is part of a relationship with a gracious and loving God.

> Having known me as the recipient of sacrifices and austerities, as the great Lord of all the worlds and the friend of all beings, he attains peace.[8]

The God to whom the ordinary worshipper offers gifts, the God who is the source and meaning of the world, is the same God who is approached and known in meditation. The *Gita*, as a part of the great Hindu epic, the *Mahabharata*, reflects and reinforces the dominant theistic tradition of Hinduism. A

Christian theologian who set out to study aspects of Hinduism at a practical level came to the conclusion that Hindu belief is best described as 'pluralistic monotheism', that is, a belief in one God who is addressed by many different names. And that astute observation confirms how a text such as the *Gita* may be used quite naturally by the Christian.[9] Bede Griffiths, writing about the same verse, said:

> Here is the teaching of the *Gita* which is also the teaching of the *Upanishads*. When one reaches the true Self, the *Atman*, the very centre of one's being, one also reaches *Brahman*, the very centre and ground of the whole creation; and that *Atman*, that *Brahman*, is the Lord and is an object of love and worship. So the whole of this yoga finally flowers in worship and love.[10]

The *Gita* provides help and advice to people who want to meditate, and in doing so it acknowledges that meditation is not a purely human-centred activity; it is practical teaching set down by people who long ago felt themselves drawn to a loving and gracious God.

But the *Gita*, although a popular and important part of scripture among Hindus, is not the main source of teaching on yoga. When I began to look at the work of Vivekananda and Aurobindo back in the late nineteen-sixties it was because of their very different responses to Western influences and their considerable contribution to the renewal of Hindu confidence and identity around the turn of the century. However, I discovered that both of them used the word 'yoga' to describe their main body of teaching. Vivekananda's most extensive work was in his lectures and writings on what he called 'Raja Yoga'; and Aurobindo gave to his lengthy and complex writings the overall description of 'Integral Yoga'. Although both men in their teaching and practice showed themselves to be masters of what in the West has usually been known as spirituality, their concerns were far wider than spiritual and physical exercises, breathing, and posture. In Hindu traditions, yoga refers to a whole school of philosophy as well as to a way of meditating. So in thinking about Vivekananda and Aurobindo, I found it necessary to read the classical text of Indian yoga, which is Patanjali's *Yoga Sutras*.

The *Yoga Sutras* were written sometime between 200 BCE and 500 CE.[11] Although they contain a good deal of other material, the most significant part is a long section called *sadhana* ('the means of attainment'). In this Patanjali sets out eight 'limbs', or stages, which are calculated to lead to the highest level of meditation. As an outline of the practice of a method of spiritual discipline and attainment, yoga has had great influence and remains one of the most important of guides, applicable in almost any religious tradition.

In the West, where yoga classes are now commonplace, they have been presented as a novel way of engaging in physical exercises, or as a method of relaxation for tense and harassed people.[12] There is nothing wrong with that. It is part of the yoga tradition. But only a part. What is offered most often in the West is *hatha yoga*,[13] that part of the system which has to do especially with control of the body, and focusses upon two or three of Patanjali's eight stages.

Properly understood, yoga is a system of strict moral, physical, mental, and spiritual training calculated to lead to deep spiritual experience and ultimately to liberation or union with God (Patanjali's teaching allowed for either alternative). People are often surprised to know that the first two stages are concerned with attitudes and behaviour, laying an ethical basis which is assumed to be essential for progress with the other steps. How popular would that be in the average yoga class, I wonder?

The first stage is described by the Sanskrit word *yama*, which means 'self-restraint'. It demands the acceptance of five 'vows', not conditioned by class, place, time, or occasion. Actually, the five are the basic ethical principles of orthodox, or high-caste, Hinduism, shared also with Jainism and, bar one, with Buddhism.[14] The first vow is *ahimsa*, or non-violence, abstaining from injury to all living things and practising gentleness towards all. The second is *satya*, or truthfulness;[15] the third *asteya*, or restraint from stealing; the fourth *brahmacarya*, or celibacy (usually understood as faithfulness within marriage and complete abstinence outside of marriage); and the fifth *aparigraha*, the absence of all kinds of covetousness or craving.

Each religious or humanistic system will have its own ethical guidelines, and it can be refreshingly surprising to find how much there is in common between people of different beliefs and different cultures. But the lesson to be drawn from *yama* is that if yoga is to be used to stimulate meditation and spiritual progress, it must rest upon a set of moral principles. In that sense, meditation cannot be separated from life in society and responsibility towards others, and the meditation itself should incorporate reflection upon such things. So the Christian yogi might ponder the significance in concrete situations of the highlighting by Jesus of the command to 'love your neighbour as yourself'.[16] The principle of *aparigraha*, or not craving, might lead to further reflection on the advice found in the Sermon on the Mount: 'Do not store up for yourselves treasures in heaven, where moth and rust destroy and thieves break in and steal.'[17] How can the idea of a simple and non-acquisitive lifestyle be applied in the frenetically materialistic world of the West? How should political and community values be adapted in conformity with this principle? And, most important question of all for the meditator, how can I adjust my own way of living in the light of this idea? One of the lessons Pöhlmann said he learned from Hindus was that:

> To be simple means not to be fraught, and to find one's way back to the elementary forms of being human – religion, family, tradition. From this perspective, to be

simple means to live naturally, not artificially, spon-
taneously, and not in an inhibited way.[18]

The first two stages of yoga remind us that meditation and
silent reflection upon our traditions do not involve rupturing
our contacts with the world around us; rather, they demand
giving serious thought to material, social, and political concerns, and to how we might play our part in influencing
them.

The second limb of Patanjali's yoga relates closely to this
theme of 'not grasping'. It is called *niyama* (limitation,
restraint), and again there are five sub-headings to flesh out
the meaning. The first is to do with purity, and in its original
context appears to have had connections with the preserva-
tion of caste purity, although it also involves purity of
thought. Then comes *samtosha*, happiness or contentment
with one's own situation. This need not imply the acceptance
of socially unjust situations, but rather the ability to accept
what cannot be changed and to work within one's own
limitations. The third sub-heading deals with austerity, and
suggests the use of deliberate self-denial in small things
(rather like the old practices of Lenten discipline or the
austerity of the Islamic Ramadan) in order to enhance the
self-discipline required to practice yoga. Fourthly there is
svadhyaya, which has to do both with reflection on one's
own life and with study of the scriptures. Finally *niyama*
advocates the surrender of the self to God – an interesting
counter to those who regard the yoga system as essentially an
atheistic one.

Already, we have seen enough in the first two stages of
yoga to provide material for many hours of meditation. Yet
this is only the foundation upon which the rest of the struc-
ture is built. And it serves as a reminder that in Christian
teaching on prayer and meditation strong links are made
between an ethical and practical grounding and the life of
prayer and devotion.[19]

The third stage of yoga is *asana*, the most familiar part of yoga practice in the West. The word means sitting down, or posture, but in yoga refers also to the physical movements, the exercises, which accompany breathing and prayer. One of the first pieces of advice given to those who would practice yoga or, say, Zen Buddhism, is to learn how to sit. Disarmingly simple, one might think. We all know how to sit. But consider the ways in which Christian worshippers arrange themselves during periods of corporate prayer. Some kneel on little cushions, elbows pressing against the shelf on the pew in front, in a posture it would be difficult to maintain for long without discomfort. Others prefer simply to bow their heads, and so slip into the nonconformist crouch – an easy position in which to go to sleep, less easy as the basis of a prolonged period of concentration. To sit comfortably for meditation one must be relaxed and able to maintain a position for a long period. That might mean sitting upright in a comfortable chair, or on a bench, feet on the floor and back straight. The Indian practice of sitting cross-legged is not necessarily a cunningly-devised esoteric posture which almost magically enhances meditation (although some yoga teachers present it this way); still less is it a device for inducing the maximum of discomfort in a search for the greatest degree of ascetic misery. It is much more simply the way that most people in rural India, accustomed to life without chairs and tables, will sit when they are relaxed to talk, or eat – and also to pray. The secret (transparent enough) of sitting is to sit in whatever way is comfortable for you if you are to remain in control of your thoughts for a lengthy period.

Asana also includes postures more dramatic than simply sitting with a straight back. The forcing of the body into strange positions (*hatha yoga*) is part of the 'physical exercise' style of yoga which is so common. But it includes different movements which can be associated with particular prayers, forming a symphony of slow deliberate movement and mental prayer which become part of the music of meditation. This stage of yoga also emphasizes the control of the body, the subduing of physical and mental distractions and the creation of a calm state of mind.

Closely linked with *asana* is the fourth stage, which is control of the breath, or *pranayama*. The main part of *pranayama* is simply the practice of breathing in, holding the breath, and breathing out. A little practice of this will give any normally healthy person the ability to hold the breath for quite long periods; to do so for a full minute is not difficult. The aim of *pranayama*, as of *asana*, is to control the body, to calm down a person's normal rush of activity and thought, to slow the pulse, and so to eliminate all sources of distraction from meditation. Deep, slow breathing is considered to be of itself an aid to concentration. In the yoga system, *pranayama* marks the point at which exercises aimed at controlling the body reach their completion.

Pranayama also uses regular breathing exercises as a framework for prayer. As a person breathes in, holds her breath for a set period, and then breathes out again (say, in a pattern of 4: 16: 8 seconds, or 5: 20: 10), so she incorporates the words of a short prayer or mantra into the rhythm of her breathing. Breathing techniques have been used in connexion with prayer in some Christian systems, and these practices can easily be linked with *pranayama*. A major text of Eastern Orthodox spirituality, the *Philokalia*, contains the advice:

> You know, brother, how we breathe; we breathe the air in and out. On this is based the life of the body and on this depends its warmth. So, sitting down in your cell, collect your mind, lead it into the path of the breath along which the air enters in, constrain it to enter the heart altogether with the inhaled air, and keep it there. Keep it there, but do not leave it silent and idle; instead give it the following prayer, 'Lord, Jesus Christ, Son of God, have mercy upon me.'[20]

It is a practice already incorporated into Christian prayer, but the yoga tradition may help us to use it with greater benefit. There are many short prayers which can accompany the rhythm of breathing and change of posture, and serve as Christian equivalents to the Hindu *mantra*. Some of the following short prayers may be found suitable:

O God, of your goodness, give me yourself, for only in you have I all.

You have made us for yourself, and our hearts are restless until they rest in you.

Help me to relax, to rest, to become open and receptive to you . . .
   Lord, I lie open before you, waiting for your leading, your peace, and your word.

From the unreal lead me to the real, from darkness lead me to light, from death lead me to eternal life.[21]

Or even more briefly,

Come, Holy Spirit.

Many more short prayers can be found, from many traditions, for this sort of use. They need not be spoken, but can be rehearsed mentally while practising breathing techniques. The association of short prayers with rhythmic breathing may well help to promote concentration and quiet.
   Another brief prayer which has a long history of use among Christians and has become popular again in recent years is the 'Jesus Prayer', quoted above from the *Philokalia*, frequently used in connection with the rhythm of breathing, and sometimes shortened to become simply the repetition of the one word, 'Jesus'. Recent Benedictine meditation,

especially that associated with John Main, has made use of
two Aramaic words (often written together as though they
were one) as a Christian *mantra*, the words *Maran atha*
('Come, Lord') repeated slowly and rhythmically with equal
stress on each syllable.[22] Graham Smith suggests the use of a
sequence of single words related to a yogic pattern of breathing: *ruah* (Hebrew for 'spirit') on breathing in; 'awake'
(recalling verses which begin, 'awake, awake, put on
strength', from Isaiah 51 and 52) while holding the breath;
and *abba* ('father') on breathing out: then *ruah*, Jesus,
rabboni ('my teacher'), and so on.[23]

In all these and other ways, the practice of brief prayers
accompanying the regular and calm breathing of *pranayama*
can help people to focus the mind, and so to move from the
more physical stages of yoga to the final four limbs. At this
stage one is invited to pass into areas associated with more
serious meditation and contemplation. If that sounds too
difficult or demanding, it may be reassuring to know that
there are simple and straightforward parts of yoga teaching
here that can be applied quite simply to prayer and reflection
at almost any level. The fifth part of Patanjali's yoga goes by
a name which means withdrawal. The Sanskrit word has
been used of the retreat of troops from battle, but more
commonly suggests the withholding of the mind from objects
of sense experience.[24] That may appear to be a tall order. But
put simply, it is an attempt to rid the mind of distractions.
Just as the yogi has by this stage gained control over her body
and minimised physical distractions, so now she tries to
do something similar with her mind. Part of the process of
relaxation and reflection is to rid the mind of ideas and
images which run around our heads like traffic on a busy
motorway. How might that be done? Perhaps the important
thing is not to be too anxious about it and thereby stimulate
the very business of the mind one is trying to avoid. William
Johnston quotes some wise words of a Zen Buddhist teacher:

When you are practising *zazen* (meditation) do not try to stop yourself thinking. Let it stop by itself. If something comes into your mind, let it come in and let it go out. It will not stay long. When you try to stop thinking, it means you are bothered by it. Do not be bothered by anything.[25]

From a Christian perspective Johnston adds the advice that it may be helpful slowly and deliberately to repeat a few words of Jesus from the Sermon on the Mount: 'Do not be anxious . . . do not be anxious'.[26] The point is to allow the mind to become free from its many distractions. Having first relaxed the body, become aware of breathing and regulated it, a person then reaches the stage at which her mind relaxes and begins to shed preoccupations and anxieties. That is *pratyahara*.

The sixth part of this yoga, *dharana* (concentration) is intimately linked with the process of stilling the mind, and for many people the two phases may be indistinguishable.[27] *Dharana* has been defined as 'the concentration of the mind within a limited mental area', and the activity of focusing or concentrating the mind is at the heart of yoga, as it is central to many other activities. The ability to shut out distractions and concentrate on the business in hand is invaluable in whatever we do: learn a language, play a sport, study a new subject; the person who can concentrate will be able to do it better. It is no different with prayer and meditation. From attempting to rid the mind of distractions we move almost imperceptibly to concentration upon an object, which may be the flame of a candle, a flower, or a religious symbol such as a cross. The object we focus on may also be a short phrase, of the kind used to accompany breathing, as stages four, five and six of Patanjali's yoga all come together. If words are used, they should not be used in a discursive kind of way but uncritically and as a means of focusing the mind. A suitable Christian mantra at this stage might be St Paul's description of the 'gifts of the Spirit':

the harvest of the Spirit is
    love, joy, peace,
    patience, kindness, goodness,
    faithfulness, gentleness and self-control.[28]

Or consistently with Quaker worship, which I guess
includes much silent reflection on social and political issues,
the ethical principles of *yama* could be mentally rehearsed:
how could non-violence, lack of covetousness, truthfulness,
and the rest be more clearly expressed in my life, or through
my influence in the world around me? Whatever the object of
concentration, the mind should now be stilled and focused,
as relaxed and controlled as the body.

This leads to meditation itself, for which the word in the
yoga system is *dhyana*, derivatives of which mean 'lost in
thought' or 'absorbed in thought'. There is an understanding
that at this stage the yogi has shed the need to try to quieten
the mind; that there is an 'uninterrupted flow of the mind
towards the object' of contemplation.[29] In the Christian
mystical tradition a distinction has been drawn between an
earlier stage of meditation, which might include concentration upon an object, and contemplation as the infusion of the
mind with joy and fulfilment and love. St John of the Cross
wrote: 'Contemplation is nothing else but a sweet, tender,
and loving infusion of God, which, if we oppose no obstacles,
inflames the soul in the spirit of love.'[30]

There is a similarity between *dhyana* and what the
Christian mystical tradition has called the Prayer of Quiet, or
the Prayer of Simplicity, in spite of the fact that St Teresa and
others thought of that prayer as preceding contemplation.
Evelyn Underhill suggested that the Prayer of Quiet is
characterized by

. . . an immense increase in the receptivity of the self, and
by an almost complete suspension of the reflective powers
. . . [The self] can no longer 'take notes': it can only

surrender itself to the stream of an inflowing life, and to the direction of a larger will.[31]

For the Christian yogi, the seventh stage of *dhyana* may lead to a level of meditation at which the grace of God becomes wedded to the activity of contemplation. That in turn leads into the final limb of yoga, that of *samadhi*, a word which in Indian traditions assumes the losing of any sense of the self as a separate object from God or from the absolute reality of *Brahman*. Precisely where the final stages of this kind of meditation lead is perhaps less important than encouraging the practice of meditation in as complete a way as possible. For prayer and meditation, properly understood, is not an activity to take people out of the ordinary everyday world into some other imagined existence; it is a way of reflecting upon daily life and human events in a way which will encourage and undergird action. Ben Okri, writing of the power of words, said:

> We should return to pure contemplation, to sweet medita-tion, to the peace of silent loving, the serenity of deep faith, to the stillness of deep waters . . . and dream good new things for humanity . . . Then maybe one day, after much striving, we might well begin to create a world justice and a new light on this earth that could inspire a ten-second silence of wonder – even in heaven.[32]

One of the great values for Christians of an acquaintance with yoga is that it reconnects them with their own ancient traditions, and helps them to graft meditation on to their own more typically activist practices. There is no contra-diction between silent reflection and the application of religious faith to social and community concerns; no neces-sary dichotomy between what have been regarded as the distinctive religious forms of mysticism and prophetic proclamation. New Testament writing on the whole seems to pay little attention to prayer and meditation – although in the midst of the complex symbolism of the book of Revelation there occurs the thought that there was 'silence in heaven for about half an hour'.[33] Significantly, the Gospel story sets the beginning of the ministry of Jesus against a moment of insight akin to what the mystic might experience. But first there is the ethical and prophetic element. The public work of Jesus is preceded by an encounter with John the Baptist, whose uncompromising preaching and vigorous denunciation of the rich and powerful attracted widespread attention and provoked inevitable opposition. That theme was quickly taken up by Jesus when he borrowed some words of the prophet Isaiah, and applied them to what he was about to do:

> he has sent me to announce good news to the poor,
>   to proclaim release for prisoners
> and recovery of sight for the blind;
>   to let the broken victims go free,
> to proclaim the year of the Lord's favour.[34]

Between the meeting with John the Baptist and that announcement came the flash of insight and then a period of silent reflection. All three synoptic gospels[35] suggest that it was at the time of his baptism by John that Jesus had a great mystical experience, as he became conscious of his awesome calling and destiny.[36] Immediately after that experience Jesus went off into the desert for a long period to be alone with his thoughts, his doubts, and his reflections on his calling. That wilderness experience was emulated by many Christians in the first few centuries of Christian faith. Origen (c. 185–254) adopted an allegorical interpretation of scripture in which the wandering of the children of Israel in the wilderness was likened to the experience of Christians who abandoned the ordinary life of the world for the solitude of the desert. The tradition developed among Christians of withdrawing to isolated places in order to live a life of prayer and poverty.

This led to the gradual establishment of small communities, and by the middle of the fourth century

> the Egyptian desert was quite heavily populated with ascetic communities, varying in style from the very tightly-organized monastic townships established by Pachomius in Upper Egypt to the looser federation of smallish groups in the north.[37]

The practices of the desert ascetics were partly modelled on the glimpses the Gospels give of Jesus going away from his disciples, and sometimes from crowds of followers, to pray and reflect and be silent.[38] The Gospels contain many examples of Jesus at prayer, Jesus silent, and Jesus in solitude, and that has inspired Christian traditions quite as much as have more active pictures of his life. Meditation and reflection belong with social action and community concerns in balanced Christian practice, just as they did in the life of Jesus.

The desert was an important location for early Christian practice of meditation. But it was in more verdant settings in monastic communities between the twelfth and fifteenth centuries that mystical life flowered in Europe, culminating in the sixteenth century in the lives of some of the most influential of Christian mystics. St Teresa of Avila (1515–1582) systematized the results of her own spiritual experience in the *Interior Castle*, using that familiar feature of the mediaeval landscape as an allegory for the progress of the soul from the outer courtyard through to the innermost of the castle's seven mansions. These stages she called the Purgative Way, the Prayer of Recollection, the Prayer of Quiet, the Prayer of Union, Ecstasy, and Spiritual Marriage. The fact that some parallels can be drawn between Patanjali's yoga and St Teresa's system does not mean that there was Indian influence on her; rather it suggests that common ground exists in matters of prayer, spirituality and mysticism between people of different faiths.

A contemporary of St Teresa's was St John of the Cross, who met St Teresa in 1567 and was encouraged by her to promote reform within the Carmelite order to which he belonged. The best-known of his contributions to the literature of Christian spirituality is *The Dark Night of the Soul*. In that book St John distinguished between active and passive aspects of meditation: the active involved both preparation for contemplation and the achievement of the union with God described by St Teresa as Spiritual Marriage; the passive – the dark night – was the experience both intellectually and in prayer of the absence of God. St John regarded the 'dark night' as an inevitable part of the spiritual path. The sense of the 'absence' of God, or of any kind of external support or encouragement, he saw as a necessary prelude to the 'dawn' of fulfilment, union, or enlightenment.[39]

A third great figure of the sixteenth century who had a profound effect on Christian thinking about prayer and the practice of meditation was St Ignatius Loyola, the Basque soldier who became the founder of the Society of Jesus and author of *The Spiritual Exercises*. The *Exercises* grew out of the pattern of reflection and prayer that Ignatius developed for his own, and then for the Jesuits', use. In his own reading Ignatius made a point of noticing his own reactions to what he read. In that way he unconsciously reflected what Buddhists call 'mindfulness', or being aware of what one is doing at every moment as part of a continual process of meditation: 'When you are walking, know that you are walking.'[40] Ignatius also taught the value of reading scripture in an imaginative way in order 'to be present through the imagination . . . but in such a way that I may actually take part in what occurs'.[41] The emphasis upon the use of the Bible brings us full circle. Increasingly, Christian meditators have been returning to the Bible as basic material for their reflection. But the difficulties of doing that without at the same time becoming immersed in the critical questions which are inevitably involved in any intelligent use of such a complex and varied body of texts are considerable. Meditation should be a way of focusing the mind, not of letting it run around searching for a way of constructing meaning out of obscure texts. The method of St Ignatius has in it much that is of use; but it could be even more valuable if its use were to be informed by insights from Hindu and Buddhist sources.

Compared with some of the traditions of Buddhism and Hinduism it may be the case that Christianity has been content to leave meditation too much to specialists in monasteries and the religious orders. Although the monastic tradition may seem to have been too dominant in some forms of the Therevada, Buddhist teaching as a whole has retained a strong sense of the central importance of meditation. The idea of 'focusing the mind' in a particular way and purifying it of obsessional thinking in order to be able to concentrate and meditate has remained a vital part of Buddhist practice. Raimundo Panikkar claimed that: 'In a certain sense we might say that Buddhism is purely and simply a school of prayer . . . as interior contemplation.'[42]

In so far as that is true, it should help Christians to regard Buddhist meditation practices as helpful aids to their own prayer. Certainly it is the case that people of all faith and none can learn from one another's experience. And the delightful thing about it is that techniques and insights used in prayer and meditation may be borrowed and lent across the boundaries which divide religions without there necessarily being any threat to a particular faith practised within its own cultural, social or historical context. Here, more than anywhere, people of different persuasions may share with one another to their mutual benefit.

The use of appropriate biblical passages, simple prayers, or Christian 'mantras', used in conjunction with insights drawn from yoga or from Buddhist practices might well lead to new interest in and excitement about systems of prayer, reflection and meditation. Such things can be developed for the use of individuals or small groups, and suitably adapted, can become part of the worship of congregations. One of the criticisms which can be made of much current Christian worship is that it allows far too few opportunities for the use of silence, and imposes far too much by way of exhortation, unexplained doctrine, or banal advice. The creative use of silence and of guided meditation might encourage people to feel that in going to church they can engage seriously in worship that has within it space for sustained reflection and real opportunities for their own spiritual growth.

3

Atheists, Agnostics and Believers

'God' is one of those slippery words which defy definition. Everybody knows what the word means until asked to explain it. Confident analysts frame their questionnaires, and then read responses to such hugely over-simplified questions as 'Do you believe in God?' to reassure churchgoers and politicians that more than seventy per cent of the population continues to believe in God.[1] How many of the respondents, I wonder, are ever perverse or precise enough to ask, 'What do you mean by "God"?' Or perhaps the simple answers reflect our weary resignation with that unassailable fact of modern life: questionnaire-speak can only exist by denying subtlety and infinite variety. As it is when used by the wily advocate in court, so it is in this case. 'Yes' or 'no' is a most convenient way of concealing the truth.

It is not only believers who labour under the illusion that confusing answers to impossible questions tell us all we need to know. Many a decent, upright atheist can be provoked to scorn by the apparent equivocation of 'it depends what you mean by "God"'. The clear denial of belief is as much in need of certainty about what is being denied as is the simple believer's affirmation about the object of faith. If belief in God is not necessarily the superstitious, somebody-out-there-will-help-me, kind of thing the atheist often supposes, what becomes of his atheism?

The impression often given in hymn and song, in sermon and testimony, of God as a superperson who meets all our needs and heals all our wounds is a convenient parody for the unbeliever to mock. And in spite of the undeniable comfort it gives to less thoughtful believers, it is also very damaging to religious belief. Believers and unbelievers alike are right to challenge the simplistic view of God as rather like the chap next door, only kinder and more malleable. Such a view is inconsistent with the general tenor of belief in the Bible, where God is pictured as powerful and aweful, inescapable but terrifying as well as, on the lips of Jesus, 'your Father in heaven'. Yet even from the lips of Jesus there comes the salutory reminder that such a father is not to be thought of simply as the bestower of benefits, for he 'causes the sun to rise on good and bad alike, and sends the rain on the innocent and the wicked'.[2] Belief in God, in other words, does not necessarily ensure rewards, or good fortune, or success. The bad and the wicked may receive good things; the good and the innocent may not. Such is the perplexing yet undeniably biblical view of God. And there is a strong strand in Christian traditions which asserts that the word God stands for something which cannot be limited by space, or time, or body; that taking the mysterious, transcendent God seriously cannot be consistent with speaking of him lightly, or carelessly.

An acquaintance with Indian religions may lead to more appropriate ways of thinking and speaking about God. Among educated Hindus, belief in one God is common, even though the religious world of the Hindu appears to be populated with many gods. Hinduism, of course, has its fair share of popular and even crude ideas about God and the gods. But educated Hindus seem to have a clearer understanding than many educated Christians of both the problems and the possibilities of speaking about God.

One of the things that has impressed me in conversations with Hindus is the way in which many of them combine a firm belief in God with an apparently sophisticated understanding of the nature of God.[3] They appreciate that when we speak of God we are not referring simply to a separate being over against ourselves; to a superperson who may act in the unpredictable and unreasonable ways that many of us do from time to time. They recognize that to use the Tamil or Sanskrit words for 'God' is to speak of a personal God who is more than just a person, for it is to invoke a name which in Indian religious traditions has served to designate both an ineffable absolute reality and a deeply personal God of grace and love. Is it surprising to realize that this is consistent with some Christian thinking about God? Can we rediscover essential but largely forgotten Christian ideas by reflecting upon Hindu teaching? Perhaps if we set aside, so far as it is possible, Christian and Western preconceptions and peep through a lens into Indian traditions we shall find ourselves enriched by the view that appears before us.

Developments in Indian thought about God, the divine, or ultimate reality, reveal provocative ideas and possible ways of thinking that can help to deepen a Christian understanding of God. How did these developments come about in a religious culture which sometimes spoke of 330 million gods?[4] A quick skip through Hindu scriptures indicates a gradual and coherent development of ideas about God. In the earliest of the Vedic writings gods appear to have been perceived in very personal terms, as heroes, or simply as the forces of the natural world.[5] There was *Indra*, the god of war and storm; *Varuna*, the over-arching sky which looked down and saw all the deeds of men and women; *Agni*, the god of fire, and fire itself; *Suriya*, the sun, bringing warmth and life to the world; *Usha*, the fresh beauty of the dawn. These gods were like people. They were capricious; they could be dangerous; it was wise to humour them. Some people – and not only among Hindus – still think of God or the gods in these ways. But for Hindus the early ideas have been infused with more profound concepts, drawn from developing traditions. Ideas changed between the construction of the earlier *Vedas* and the *Brahmanas*. People began to ask, 'what, if anything, lies behind these many gods?' 'Is there some great power or principle to which even the gods are subject?' It is in the *Upanishads* that we see some of the conclusions to which those questions led.

The *Upanishads* articulated thoughts about a reality (called *Brahman*) which is believed to be the source and meaning of the whole world. *Brahman* is a difficult word to translate. Perhaps it is best rendered as 'ultimate reality'. Hindus sometimes use *Brahman* as another word for God; only *Brahman* suggests something much more profound than the gods who appear and act in the world, to whom names can be given. The very use of the word *Brahman* indicates that what is in the mind of the speaker is not a person who may or may not act to help you; who may listen to your pleas, answer your prayers, and be generally accommodating. *Brahman* rather suggests ideas of 'whatever it is that gives meaning and purpose to the world and to our lives'.

Actually, *Brahman* has been thought of in two ways. In positive terms it is possible to attribute three qualities to *Brahman* – existence (*sat*); consciousness (*chit*); and bliss (*ananda*). *Brahman* is existence, consciousness and bliss. But against that, the *Upanishads* also admit that anything said of *Brahman* must be inadequate or misleading. For the thought *Brahman* struggles to express is one that is difficult if not impossible to put into words. Whatever we say of *Brahman*, it is never quite that. However we conceive of the ultimate reality, it is always going to be greater than our minds can grasp. Here Indian religious writing was expressing a concept employed later in Christian traditions, when thinkers of the early church, Christian mystics, mediaeval, and some modern theologians have spoken and written of God in what are called apophatic terms. That is, they have said that God can only be described in negatives, for whatever is said of God, he is always too vast and mysterious to be comprehended. Our words about God are at best allusions, hints, rumours. What God is we cannot express. The development of those early Indian writings led to a conclusion reached independently by some Christian thinkers, whose thoughts would probably astonish most devout and practising Christians. So is that one thing the traditions of the East may lead us to? – the rediscovery of legitimate but seldom-used ways for Christians to think about God? Recalling the words of an early Christian writer, Dionysius, Raimundo Panikkar wrote: ' "If someone, seeing God, knew what he saw, he did not see God", said Denis the Areopagite, and with him the greatest part of Christian tradition.'[6]

Could it be that the idea of God admits of broader understandings than many people in the Western world currently assume, and that the subtle thinking of such Indian writing as the *Upanishads* may reconnect us with our own traditions?

It was during the period of 500 years or so in which the *Upanishads* were being written that Buddhism arose in India.[7] It was a time of much questioning of received religious teaching. There was dissatisfaction with the control of religious rites by the *brahmins*.[8] Along with that went a wider questioning of belief, which included critical attitudes to the over-personalized gods of the early Vedas and subsequent reflection about *Brahman*, or ultimate reality, which found expression in the *Upanishads*. In Budddhist teaching, too, there was a deliberate turning-away from the predominant sacrificial and ritual concerns of 'Brahmanism'. It is said that the Buddha declined to discuss the question of God, neither affirming nor denying his existence, and regarding metaphysical discussion as an unnecessary distraction from the more serious business of pursuing enlightenment. The earliest Buddhism of north-eastern India appears to have been a human-centred religion, in that there was no reference to God or the gods, no teaching about a saviour, and no recourse to supernatural agencies. In the course of time Buddhism developed most of the features of thought and practice that we think of as 'religious', although the considerable appeal of Buddhism in the West today does seem to relate to its ability to provide ways of religious practice without reference to the supernatural. Christians need not regard that as a negative, still less a hostile, feature. In his often provocative but remarkably profound book, Raimundo Panikkar explored ideas that emerge out of the Christian apophatic tradition in the light of Buddhist teaching. He asked: '. . . can there be an atheistic religion? The Buddha's answer is trenchant. Only an atheist religion can actually be a religion. All the rest is idolatry, the worship of a God who is the work of our hands or our minds.'[9]

God is a word for a mystery; for something that constantly eludes the attempt of the human mind to grasp it. Neat definitions and descriptions of God may serve some purpose as signposts, but they must not be confused with the reality to which they point. The wisdom of Christian apophatic, Buddhist and much Hindu teaching is that it reminds us that God is always more than our minds can grasp or our thoughts conceive.

There are parallels to be drawn between developments in India of ideas of God, from the early *Vedas* to the *Upanishads* and Buddhism, and developments over a shorter period in early Christianity. It is clear that in the first three centuries of Christian history a wide variety of beliefs and interpretations co-existed within Christian communities. The process of church councils gradually coming to agreement about what should constitute an orthodox position was a long one. Not until late in the fourth century were definitions formally agreed in ways that made it possible to identify heretics and to draw boundaries of 'correct' belief around the church. Some would see that process as a proper and necessary one, enabling all Christians to be clear about what their basic beliefs should be. The setting out of the creeds provided agreed formulas of belief.[10] In the twentieth century the Nicene creed has been regarded as a basic statement which could provide a common platform for the never-quite-realized progress towards church unity. Creeds do provide common statements; but of course, they have to be interpreted. There can be little doubt that even within single con-gregations the interpretations made by individuals as to what words of the creeds might mean will differ widely. It can be argued that the imposition of a kind of orthodoxy in the late fourth century was an unfortunate attempt to impose the views of one party and to close off further development of ideas among Christians in ways that did not happen, for example, in India.[11]

Of course, there is always a need for popular religion which conveys in picture-language beliefs about a transcen-dent reality and the significance of faith, hope and love in a matter-of-fact world. India provides stunning examples of popular religion, filled with colour and noise, fanciful images and extravagant devotion. Even Buddhism, which in its beginnings was concerned more with meditation and morality than with ritual and the supernatural, has developed popular forms very similar to those found in Hinduism and indeed in Christianity. In Sri Lanka, one of the heartlands of 'pure' Buddhism, the religion has long accommodated a wide range of popular practices and is continuing to develop in ways that take it ever further from the Buddhism of the beginnings.[12]

Yet the popular religion which invokes the supernatural and inevitably becomes a breeding-ground for superstition and endless misconceptions needs to be balanced by a readily accessible intellectual system. Curiously, that seems to be disappearing from view in late twentieth-century Christianity, buried beneath the rubble of ill-thought out theology and morality and banal practice. The trick is to combine popular expressions of religion with more thought-ful interpretations which provide sustenance for those whose education and cultural mores make the popular diets unpalatable. The genius of Hindu and Buddhist traditions is that they have made room in a perfectly natural way for a parallel existence of the popular and the intellectual.

Astonishing as it may seem to many modern-day

Christians, Christianity contains significant echoes of that same theme. The fourth century did not put an end to the often adventurous and subtle interpretations which had been commonplace among the early Church Fathers. The great mediaeval theologian Thomas Aquinas was deeply influenced by wider cultural and intellectual traditions than his own, partly through the scholarly activities of Islam and Judaism which were alive in Spain until almost the end of the fifteenth century.[13] Moses Maimonides, a Spanish Jew greatly influenced by the ideas of Aristotle and commonly regarded as the greatest of Jewish mediaeval philosophers, adopted a rationalistic attitude towards the decalogue and miracles. This all contributed to the way in which Aquinas came to emphasize an understanding of God as 'existence itself' (*esse suum subsistens*) rather than as a separate being among other beings.

This concept of God as 'being itself' rather than as a being among other beings, susceptible of proof and emptied of mystery, is found among modern Christian theologians. One of the most creative theologians of the twentieth century, Paul Tillich, wrote in ways that suggested considerable correspondence with ideas of other religions. Tillich was convinced that 'the basic theological question is the question of God.'[14] Like Panikkar, he believed that the traditional arguments for the existence of God are self-defeating, and that many of those who follow those traditions do so in a misguided and unhelpful way.[15] God is not a being among other beings, he argued in words which (did he know it?) are reminiscent of Islam. Surah 112 of the *Qur'an* asserts: 'Equal to Him (Allah) is no one', and Falaturi commented on that: 'This kind of negative characterization attests to the unity and uniqueness of God, and therefore to radical monotheism.'[16]

The apophatic tradition in Christian thought – the idea that the concept of God is beyond human expression – is consistent with Islam, as well as with Buddhism and Hinduism.

Some Christians shy away from such comparisons, believing that they dilute the supposed purity and distinctiveness of Christian thought. The old jibe of Ronald Knox, that 'comparative religion makes people comparatively religious' still strikes a chord in many a Christian heart. People worry that their beliefs will be called into question if other people's beliefs are given serious consideration. The opposite may be more likely. As in other fields of human activity and knowledge, a correspondence of ideas over different places and periods should at least give us pause, and make us ask whether such consistency is not a possible indication of the validity of the idea.

In a phrase reminiscent of much Indian thought, Paul Tillich reminds us that God 'cannot bear the marks of finitude'.[17] What we mean by the word 'God' cannot simply be a person among other persons; a being among beings only a little more powerful; an object among all the objects in the world that could be produced on demand. Tillich suggested that when the Scholastics[18] spoke of the existence of God they meant, 'the reality, the validity, the truth of the idea of God, an idea which did not carry the connotation of *something* or *someone* who might or might not exist'.[19] It sounds alarming. But it indicates the place in the history of Christian thought of reminders, in the midst of the incessant activities of popular religion, that taking the mysterious, transcendent God seriously cannot mean speaking of him lightly and easily, as though he might be met in the street. There have always been those who have asserted that whatever we say of God is too limited, or too narrow. Our words about God are always symbols, struggling to express what is beyond human language.[20]

Here we are close to ways in which Indian religious traditions have spoken of *Brahman* – the ineffable mystery behind the universe, but also within ourselves, which paradoxically may be related to the myriad colourful gods who are the objects of worship. Modern Hinduism has been remarkably successful in holding together negative (apophatic) ways of speaking of God and popular worship. When years ago I first read the works of Swami Vivekananda, founder of the Ramakrishna Mission (the first Hindu missionary organization to win Western converts) I was struck both by his vigorous criticism of ways in which most Christians speak about God and by the alternative he offered. And in twenty-five years of teaching courses on modern Hinduism, I am repeatedly struck by the excitement his ideas can still generate in students. Vivekananda taught a form of *advaita* (non-dualism), which asserts that everything in the universe is in some sense a unity. There is only one reality (which Hindus call *Brahman*) and everything is a manifestation of that reality. As a consequence, everything and everybody is related. *Advaita*, like other major Hindu schools of thought, is partly based on the *Upanishads*, and reflects the teaching of those scriptures that the goal of the religious quest is to realize the unity between the individual self (*atman*) and the great 'Self' which is *Brahman*. It was within that idea that Vivekananda accommodated an understanding of how different kinds of religious expression relate to each other.

> The same God whom the ignorant man saw outside nature, the same whom the little-knowing man saw as interpenetrating the universe, and the same whom the sage realizes as his own Self, as the whole universe itself – all are One and the same Being, the same entity seen from different standpoints. . . perceived by different minds.[21]

Popular worship, speaking of God in terms borrowed from human relationships or personal devotion, all could be accommodated for Vivekananda – a deeply religious person – within the category of *advaita*. All genuine spirituality, prayer and worship he regarded not in stark terms of 'true' or 'false', but as legitimate if they pointed in the end to the one great reality of *Brahman*.

Vivekananda's teaching appealed to a number of Westerners, and especially to intellectuals such as Aldous Huxley, Gerald Heard, and Christopher Isherwood, who were searching for some kind of spiritual reality but had rejected what seemed to them to be the simplistic teaching of Christianity. In lectures he gave in the United States of America and in Europe Vivekananda focused on Raja Yoga, and therefore on methods of meditation and reflection. In that respect Vivekananda and early converts to the Ramakrishna Mission were foreshadowing those in the West who later were to be attracted to forms of Indian or Eastern religions – more often Buddhist in the late twentieth century – which offer training in meditation and a spiritual path to follow without requiring belief in the supernatural. In India meanwhile the Ramakrishna Mission devoted much effort to forms of social service, thus expressing another aspect of any genuine spirituality.

But, the critic may ask, is this not all far too impersonal? How is this mysterious, ineffable reality to be known? All religions have their answers to that question. For Muslims, what Allah requires is expressed chiefly through the *Qur'an*. It is the scripture which mediates Allah's word to people. For Hindus, the later *Upanishads* introduced the concept of *Ishvara*, the personal Lord, or God, who appears in the world in various forms, and may be worshipped. *Ishvara* is a manifestation of *Brahman*, an incarnation which makes known something (but not all) of his reality. There is no inconsistency between worshipping the personal Lord (perhaps in the form of *Vishnu* or *Shiva* or *Rama* or *Krishna*) and at the same time remaining aware of the absolute, ineffable *Brahman*.

For Christians the mysterious, transcendent God is made known in Jesus Christ. He it is who provides a window into the otherwise unknowable God. St Paul wrote that 'the gospel of the glory of Christ' brings light to humankind, and the word for light in the Greek is *photismos*.[22] The Christian

picture of Jesus Christ is aptly described by the word we now
use for one of the most ubiquitous products of modern tech-
nology, the photograph, literally something 'written in light'.
As the photograph is made by the image outside the camera
briefly engraving itself in light on the film, so Christian
understanding is that the life and teaching of Jesus is like a
shutter opening for a brief moment to reveal the nature of
God. The unknown God is made known in Christ.

But Christian thought relates the revelation in Christ to
other intimations of God's activity. In John's Gospel the
Greek word *logos* is used for the expression of God that has
existed since the beginning, for 'through him (the *logos*) all
things came to be'. Although most English translations
render *logos* as 'word' it means something more like
'utterance' or 'speech', and so in its New Testament context
has the sense of an intelligible divine self-disclosure. The
biblical view is that God's 'word' was instrumental in bringing the world into being – in other words, that creation was
itself an act of divine self-disclosure; that it was the 'word' of
God that was spoken by the prophets; and that finally that
same 'word' was declared in the form of Jesus of Nazareth.

The use of *logos* to describe this act of divine self-
disclosure reflects much wider cultural, philosophical and
theological contents than those of first-century Judaism and
Christianity alone. In his attempts to express an understanding of the revelation in Jesus the author of John's Gospel provided a means by which Christian belief can be related to
what occurred before the birth of Jesus and what lay beyond
his knowledge. *Logos* could convey the sense of the reason
that informs all rational human beings. In using the word for
Jesus Christ, the New Testament allows for comparisons
with the great Greek philosophers and the messages spoken
through the Jewish prophets; and it enables later interpreters
to link the story of the word made flesh in John's Gospel with
divine disclosures which may have occurred outside the
world of the Bible.

To use the concept in this way is by no means an invention of twentieth-century liberals or radicals. Early Christian writers, including Justin Martyr and Clement of Alexandria, made fruitful connections between the idea of a universal *logos* and the Christian belief in the word made flesh. And the connection suggests that what can be known directly is the *logos* not, in Christian terminology, God the Father.[23] Indeed, that thought is reinforced by the conclusion to John's prologue, which declares that: 'No one has ever seen God; God's only Son, he who is nearest to the Father's heart, has made him known.'[24]

That is consistent with Jewish belief and with Muslim insistence upon the supremacy and oneness of Allah. Christians believe that God has revealed himself in Jesus; but that is not the same as believing that Jesus is God.[25] Such careful distinctions are often overlooked by Christian congregations and preachers, but to the detriment it would seem of Christian belief as a credible faith. Years of teaching the history of religions to sceptical undergraduates who rarely had any religious or theological background convinced me that what they rejected was all too often a parody which took for granted the assumption that when Christians talk about God they are speaking only of a particular human being who lived and taught in Palestine early in the first century. Distinctions between Jesus and God need to be made more frequently and more carefully than is usually the case.

William Johnston complained about the dangers of this tendency when he wrote:

For the past few centuries popular Christianity has spoken of God in a dualistic and even anthropomorphic way. I say popular Christianity because mystics like Eckhart, the anonymous author of *The Cloud*, John of the Cross, and the rest were never guilty of this oversimplification . . . popular Christianity had the strong, if unconscious tendency to put God *in* a place, and this tendency still persists. . . . God is nowhere. He simply is.[26]

In reflecting light from other traditions on Christian faith and practice we may remember that Hindus were often criticized vigorously for their idolatry. The common European assumption about worship in India was that the use of images in worship was necessarily an indication of idolatry. The superiority of Christians by comparison seemed obvious. 'The heathen in his blindness/Bows down to wood and stone.'[27] Yet few Christians appear to have paused to ask whether Hindus are alone in using pictures, images and statues as aids to worship, what it is that constitutes idolatry, and whether Christians themselves might sometimes be guilty of it. Words are also images, as are the pictures produced in the mind by hymns and prayers. In resisting the desire to regard God as one object among many it might be the case – audacious though the thought seems – that Christians would be resisting idolatry. All idolatry in one way or another consists in stopping at the sign or symbol; whereas true religion requires not a refusal to use signs and symbols, but a willingness to pass beyond the sign to what it signifies.[28] God has no equal; no equivalent; God is beyond the categories of our minds; we speak and think of God only by way of symbols. And we approach him in response to his own disclosures of himself in the world.

The subtlety of thought about God in India – and indeed in some Christian traditions – is careful with its definitions and distinctions, but it is also vividly aware of the importance of religious experience. The *Upanishads* and the use made of their texts in *advaita* regard the goal of the religious quest as the experiential knowledge of the unity of the individual self (*atman*) and the universal reality of *Brahman*. One of the refrains of the *Upanishads* is: 'I am *Brahman*' – within me, there lives something of the ultimate reality, the Absolute, which is called *Brahman*. In meditation the individual reflects upon that astonishing claim. The immanence of *Brahman* within each individual is an important part of Hindu thought, and at many levels Hindu faith is imbued with the idea that the individual self is a microcosm of the Absolute. The transcendent God, or *Brahman*, is reflected, however dimly, within the spirit of every individual person. The *Chandogya Upanishad* puts it like this: 'Now the light which shines beyond the heavens, . . . in the highest and most exalted worlds, that is indeed the same as the light within man.'[29]

Or in an account of instruction given by a learned father to his son, who had returned home after twelve years study of the *Vedas*, 'priding himself on his learning and obdurate', but seeming not to have grasped some of the most important truths: 'This finest essence – the whole universe has it as its Self. That is the Real: That is the Self: That *you* are, Svetaketu.'[30]

In Christianity also the idea of the 'God within' has taken a central place, and has been essential to the development of Christian faith from the beginning. The belief that God is active within the personal and corporate lives of believers is as central to Christian understanding as are beliefs in the one transcendent God and in the revelation in Jesus Christ. The beginnings of Christian faith and of the church were directly related to experiences of renewal and activity which were understood by those involved as the work of the Holy Spirit, of God somehow active within them and their community. But Christian believers were in no doubt that this was part of the activity of the one God in whom they – and their Jewish brothers and sisters – believed.[31]

Just as a knowledge of a transcendent God requires revelation, through the *Qur'an*, through Christ, or through *Ishvara*, so a living experience of God requires a sense of his immanence, present and active within human lives. The sense of an indwelling power or influence, variously conceived and described, is an elemental religious feeling, common to all traditions. It may be described in terms of an 'inner light', of conscience, or as *atman*. For Christians it is in the doctrine of the Holy Spirit that ideas of the one mysterious God and of the religious sense present and active within each person meet. It allows that religious experience may be genuinely an experience of God. It concedes the possibility of divine activity being linked to human thought and will. One of the striking things about a specifically Christian understanding of this is that the activity of the Spirit always has a corporate dimension. It is not simply a matter of private experience or of heightened consciousness, but of something which is likely to relate particularly to the life of a community, and to be worked out within communities.[32]

Yet there is a deeply personal aspect to what is described by Christians as the activity of the Spirit. Much of what that means was brought out beautifully in a book by John V. Taylor. Writing of moments of recognition and awareness that seem to be activities of the Spirit, he said:

> But what is this force which causes me to see in a way in which I have not seen? What makes a landscape or a person or an idea come to life for me and become a presence towards which I surrender myself? I recognize, I respond, I fall in love, I worship – yet it was not I who took the first step. In every encounter there has been an anonymous third party who makes the introduction, acts as a go-between, makes two beings aware of each other . . . sets up a current of communication between them.[33]

Taylor's evocative presentation of the Spirit as the 'go-between', of that within us which makes us aware of beauty and truth and goodness and draws us closer to God reminds us that there is a sense in which the Spirit too is hidden. We are never directly aware of the Spirit's presence, since it is the Spirit who creates awareness. John Taylor provides a moving illustration of the activity which stimulates us and brings us to life in a re-telling of the story of Dante and Beatrice. The unrequited love of Dante, from the moment he first saw Beatrice as a young girl on a May morning in Florence until her death at the age of twenty-four, was regarded by the renaissance poet as the means of awakening stupendous creative powers within himself:

> Already my heart and will were wheeled by love;
> The Love that moves the sun and the other stars.[34]

The fact that human relationships, and especially human love, can be used so naturally and effectively as a way of explaining the activity of the Spirit is no surprise when one considers the centrality of love in a Christian understanding of God. God as love is a major part of the teaching of the New Testament, and it is occasionally spelt out in surprisingly candid ways. The First Letter of John provides a definition of God within a passage that relates an understanding of God to human relationships:

> Everyone who loves is a child of God and knows God, but the unloving know nothing of God, for God is love . . . God has never been seen by anyone, but if we love one another he himself dwells in us; his love is brought to perfection within us . . . God is love; he who dwells in love is dwelling in God, and God in him.[35]

How far this is from many doctrinally-laden definitions of God! He who loves is a child of God; the unloving know nothing of God. If we love one another, God himself dwells in us. God *is* love; he who loves dwells in God. God is to be discovered in loving relationships. Increasingly, Christians appear to be thinking of God in ways which relate to ideas of act, relationship, and love rather than to the traditional Greek formulations of substance.[36] In part that has to do with movements in both philosophy and theology, but it also reflects dissatisfaction with crude ideas of a superperson who exists in order to fulfil our desires. Reflecting upon the difficulties of believing in 'a God who will put everything right' after the terrible evil of the Holocaust, Marcus Braybrooke wrote:

> increasingly I sense that God's only power is the demand of suffering love, embodied by Jesus Christ. God makes himself one with those who suffer to appeal through them to the conscience of the world.[37]

The idea of God's power as the power of suffering love also relates to the ways of understanding God as act and relationship, rather than as substance, found in process theology. That form of Christian thought seems to many today to be more consistent with the God reflected in the gospels than is 'the immutable, impassible, static associations of the classical concept'.[38] On this understanding the word 'God' stands not only for the sense of meaning and purpose and conscience which religious believers find in their experience and in the world around them, but also for the process of love and care and concern for others which acts out that belief. The idea of God as the process of love turns out to be more challenging than the idea of God as a being. For it suggests that concern for others, whether in personal relationships or in wider affairs of peace and justice is itself the way to what is meant by 'God'. 'He who dwells in love is dwelling in God . . . the unloving know nothing of God.' In the light of those statements of faith, Christian belief shifts away from being principally a set of beliefs about some other world in some other place. It becomes much more focused upon choosing to act in a particular way, consistent with the life and teaching of Jesus Christ, and is therefore committed to the working out of a costly and sacrificial love in human relationships. It also accepts that in the tenderest experiences of human love there is a possibility of discovering at least something of what is meant by the tantalizing word 'God'.

Whatever words we use about God, they are never quite adequate. Words about God are at best symbols, clothing hints of transcendence in the coarseness of human language. However, we can say that God is not a being, not a super-person handing out rewards and punishments; what God is is much more like a pattern of meaning and purpose and a process of love and care. Such a God is revealed through mediators, which include scriptures, prophets, the natural world, and for Christians especially the life and teaching of Jesus Christ. What we mean by God is also something immanent in each person, so that there is a correspondence between a transcendent ultimate reality and the spirit, conscience and thoughts of each individual.

Christian beliefs include the convictions that God is not an object to be possessed, that he is a power rather than a property; that God is known through revelations of creativity and meaning found in great scriptures, major prophets, and inspired teachers; that God may also be known in relationships, and especially as love; and that God is an immanent power and influence within each one of us. Rightly understood and applied, these convictions could let in sufficient air to allow intellectuals to breathe, and open doors through which all may pass to glimpse some vision of the divine.

4

The Cause or Cure of Selfishness

Religion can be a very selfish activity. There is an unkind stereotype of Christians who use the organization of the churches as a vehicle for an ego trip which is not available to them elsewhere. Some seem to find an illusion of importance in even the smallest and most marginalized of church organizations. And there are those for whom even the most charitable of activities appears to be clothed with an air of smug self-satisfaction or infected by self-justification. Don Cupitt neatly summed up the second of these when he wrote of religious believers concealing their inner despair by living for others: 'and the irony of their situation makes them the subject of many jokes. "She lives for others, and you can tell the others by their hunted looks" '.[1] Those of us who have worked in churches can recognize the occasional realities behind the caricature. Religion can be the cause of selfishness.

On the other hand, religious commitment can encourage unselfishness and a regard for the good of others. The remarkable level of tolerance and forgiveness shown by Nelson Mandela to his former opponents, in so far as that reflects the influence of Christian faith in his make up, is one example of those things. When John Robinson wrote his theological best-seller, *Honest to God*, he gave the title 'The Man for Others' to a chapter which portrayed Jesus as one who was remarkable chiefly for his willingness to live for others rather than for his own self-interest, and he commended that as an example to be followed by Christians.

Robinson quoted with evident approval the comment of Dietrich Bonhoeffer that: 'Christians range themselves with God in his suffering; that is what distinguishes them from the heathen.'[2]

As an observation about what might be historically or sociologically true, that seems very wide of the mark. But as an expression of an ideal to which Christians might aspire, it is both striking and challenging. But can it be done without collapsing Christian living into a dreary diet of defeatism and martyrdom?

One way or another most great religious traditions have been concerned with the question of how to handle the self; how to reconcile instinctive human drives to survive and succeed with religious and moral teaching about self-restraint. Naked egotism is widely – although not universally – recognized as socially damaging as well as personally unpleasant, and it seems in any case to be at odds with common religious teaching about subordinating oneself to a higher power or a transcendent goal. There is something about the person who has truly understood and appropriated the best of a religious tradition which in this respect is both recognizable and attractive. It was impossible to meet Bede Griffiths without being impressed by his serenity and his evident spirituality. To a lesser degree the same was true of my Hindu friends in Vellore. They were well educated and professional people, but they certainly were not rich. Their lives had not yielded more than very modest material comforts. Yet they appeared to be content, at ease with themselves and with other people. They were not boastful or arrogant. Indeed, an attractive element about the best of Indian lives, seen in Griffiths as well as among many Hindus, was a kind of natural modesty and humility. I recall that at the time of the Beatles' visit to their guru in northern India I asked one of the *brahmins* in our study group what he thought of the publicized and packaged guru who had attracted such a famous Western following. He smiled gently, and replied:

'If a man is truly a guru, people will find their own way to him.'

That conviction revealed a profound sense of the difference between outward appearance and inner reality which seemed to be a natural part of the best of Hindu traditions, as it is also of Buddhism. Evidently, religious practice can provide a cure for selfishness. But for Christians in the West, it may be particularly difficult to recognize that. We live in societies which are strongly permeated by the values of marketing and advertising, in which appearances are thought to be all-important. It is not easy for religion to be insulated from that climate. Some of the best known and most admired exponents of Christianity have been those who have been especially skilled in presentation. Even a popular musical picked that up in caricaturing American values by including a reference to a well known Protestant preacher and writer of the nineteen-fifties and sixties in a line of a song which ran: 'Dr Norman Vincent Peale, tells you how you ought to feel.' Telling people how to feel good; assuring them that they are good people (by comparison with others outside the congregation); encouraging them to be self-satisfied; these are tricks of the trade of many a successful priest or minister. And given the difficulties of the job they are required to do, how could one blame them for recognizing that, and capitalizing on it? And yet . . . is there not a conflict between that and living as a man, or woman, for others; between that and being able to recognize the differences between outward appearance and inner reality ; between the smug self-satisfaction it may induce, and the serenity and evident spirituality of those who seem best to represent the positive values of religion?

Given the overwhelming influence and long ascendancy of market-orientated thinking in the West, it may be that the religions of the East still have valuable things to teach us about how to handle the self, and how to balance the demands of proper self-expression and self-development on the one hand and destructive self-assertion on the other. The religions of India are deeply concerned about how to handle the self. It could be argued that this is the crux of much Hindu and Buddhist teaching. Buddhism pays great attention to questions of how to understand the self; how to come to terms with oneself; how in the end to overcome or lose all self-concern. In many Hindu traditions detachment from material or worldly concerns is regarded as a state of mind which must be cultivated if liberation is to be achieved. It is attachment to our own selfish interests and desires which, according to the law of *karma*, causes people's rebirth. It would not be an exaggeration to say that the problem of overcoming selfishness, and subordinating egotism and self-concern to some greater concern or goal, is among the three or four major issues addressed by all the great religions.

In the New Testament, teaching on this theme may appear to be hidden within – or subordinated to – more overtly doctrinal Christian concerns. Difficult and controversial doctrines about the atonement and taking up the cross conceal from the view of many Christians what might be much more straightforward ideas about self-restraint. Nevertheless, teaching about the need to control the self and to overcome selfish inclinations is central to the teaching of Jesus as recorded in the Gospels. To read texts about the renunciation of the self with half on eye on what other faiths have to say on the subject could help Christians to see such teaching in a new and valuable light, and in a way that can supplement without setting aside the more traditional interpretations. What is written on the flyleaf may suggest fresh insights into what are increasingly difficult ideas for many Christians. So what may we find to help us in the religious traditions of the East?

In Buddhism, handling and overcoming the attachment and desires which build up our selfish inclinations is a fundamental objective. Of course, Buddhism varies enormously in the forms it takes and the beliefs and practices it incorporates. But running through all the varieties is a concern to deal with the self, and to subjugate egotism in the pursuit of liberation. Central to Buddhist teaching, and especially important in early Buddhist teaching in India, is the cultivation of an awareness of the impermanence of all things. According to the doctrine of *anicca* (impermanence), the most important fact about our world and ourselves is that everything is constantly changing. One of the illusions to which our senses and our human conditioning subject us is that the objects we perceive in the world around us are unchanging, permanent realities. We look out on the world and assume that what we see is a reality that lasts. The grass beneath our feet, the pattern of the stars in the sky, the level of the trees on the horizon, the gentle sweep of the coastline, are all taken by our initial sense perception to be a permanent, abiding reality. Yet when we think about it, we recognize that it is not so. Our bit of land was once joined to a larger continent. How could that have been, and we had not noticed! It seems astonishing just to contemplate such a fact. The stars in the sky will not be seen in quite the same way by generations that follow us; indeed, what we now see may have changed beyond recognition in the light years that intervene between a distant star and what we see from our own time and place. It seems to me amazing that were there to be someone with a sufficiently powerful telescope somewhere out on another planet, they could look at earth and see, say, my long-dead grandparents roaming the streets of London as young children; or from a more distant place, could at this very moment look and see a world in which human beings had not yet emerged. This is no longer imagination, but physics.

What we perceive through our five senses is not necessarily what is actually there. And this thought has always been a part of Buddhist teaching, expressed in different ways, of course, at different times. The Buddha, in sixth- or fifth-century India, reflected on the nature of reality, and concluded that everything changes, nothing abides. This, he declared, is an absolutely essential fact to recognize if we are to understand the world and our place in it. Further, our ideas about *ourselves* will be plagued by deception if we do not acknowledge the simple fact that we and all about us are in a state of constant change.

There is a simple story about the early life of the Buddha which is used to illustrate the essential truth that everything changes. It is said that Gautama, who became the Buddha, was brought up in comfort and ease in a princely household in the north-east of India. The story has it that at his birth a soothsayer predicted that Gautama would have a happy and successful life as a prince provided that he did not see certain signs of human suffering. Were that to happen, he would become a *sannyasi*. Alarmed by the warning, his parents went to great lengths to protect him. But one day, when he was in his late twenties, Gautama escaped from the restrictions placed upon him and had himself driven out of the palace and through the town. There he saw four things that made him think furiously.

The first was an old man, wrinkled and bent. Unexceptionable as this may seem, it led Gautama to reflect upon the inevitability of ageing. In spite of his privileges, and regardless of anything he might do, he would grow old. His physical form would change and decay. Nothing could prevent that. The second sight that drove home the fact of impermanence was a visibly ill man. Gautama recognized that his own good health would not last indefinitely; he would not always be able to rely on his physical health and vigour. The third thing he saw was a corpse being carried through the streets to the cremation ground. It was a reminder that everybody dies, and that no amount of wealth and power can prevent that inevitable destiny. Life itself is the most surely impermanent thing of all. Gautama realized that, however hard he might try, he could not succeed in clinging to life, or health, or wealth.

The fourth sight he saw that day was a wandering ascetic, a *sannyasi* who had renounced the world in order to find liberation from the round of birth and death. Gautama resolved that he, too, would renounce his privileges, his family and all that he had. He would set out as a wandering ascetic to try to find how to come to terms with a world of constant change. That night he left the palace, his wife and young son, and embarked upon a life of renunciation. Years later, he discovered the 'Middle Way' to peace and liberation, and woke up in his enlightenment as the Buddha.

The story (and most Buddhists would be indifferent as to whether or not it could be regarded as historically true) vividly describes the central problem identified by Buddhism. The fact that everything changes, and that there is nothing permanent or enduring to cling to, is a real problem for people whose lives consist largely of attempts to satisfy their cravings for things that are actually impermanent. What, then, can we cling to?

The question, posed particularly sharply by Buddhism, is one addressed in various ways by all the great religions. In the Hebrew Bible the Psalmist laments:

> seventy years is the span of our life,
> eighty if our strength holds out;
> . . . for they pass quickly and we vanish.[3]

For Jews, Christians and Muslims hope resides in an eternal God who endures though all else changes. The sixteenth century Christian mystic, Teresa of Avila, expressed that hope in a poem:

> Everything passes, all is denied.
> Everything passes, God will abide.[4]

Unlike Judaism, Christianity and Islam, however, Buddhism in its early Indian form did not encourage people to believe in a personal God; it is said that the Buddha refused to discuss the question of God, regarding it as unhelpful to what essentially had to be done by men and women if they were to come to terms with their situation. So the 'Four Noble Truths' which summarize basic ideas of Therevada Buddhism teach that all life is unsatisfactory (the Pali word *dukkha*, used in the Four Noble Truths, is often translated as 'suffering'; it seems to me that 'unsatisfactoriness' conveys the sense better). This unsatisfactoriness is said to be the result of craving (*tanha*) for things which cannot last and which therefore cannot satisfy us other than temporarily. The way to overcome *dukkha* is to 'let go', to stop desiring the things that in the end we cannot have.

This may sound a very negative doctrine. Hope for nothing, and if nothing is what you get you will not be disappointed. Don't get attached to anyone; that way, your friends and acquaintances can never let you down. Such a negative reading of the teaching of the Four Noble Truths would be mistaken. The teaching is part of a more profound understanding both of the human condition and of what is required of a workable religious system. It has to do with a way of practising a proper kind of disinterest (which is not the same as being uninterested) whilst being engaged in the struggles and contradictions, the elation and despair of daily life in the world. The Noble Truths suggest that we must recognize the transient nature of the world around us, and by doing that refuse to be attached to those things we cannot hold on to indefinitely. There is something slightly comic or pathetic about a person whose life is focused solely on remaining forever young. It is one thing to keep in good physical condition, to exercise and eat sensibly, and to take care of one's health. It is quite another to be paranoid about retaining a youthful vigour which in the very nature of things slips steadily from our grasp. Gasps of panic at the first grey hairs; desolation when a favourite walk takes ten minutes longer than once it did; denial of another birthday and another milestone passed – all these things are signs of a trivial and undeveloped understanding of who and what we are. Buddhist teaching would have us recognize reality, and then get on with doing what has to be done, both in the development of our own particular skills and talents and in the contributions we can make to the communities of which we are part. Disinterested action is action performed without selfish motives; doing good for the sake of the act itself, and for the people it influences, not for our own sakes. Disinterested action means remaining impartial to praise or blame, gain or loss, in following our proper moral and religious paths.

The Buddhist emphasis on impermanence is not restricted to external objects in the natural world or to relationships. It also influenced Buddhist understanding of the self. Everything changes. And that 'everything' includes our self. In Buddhist teaching about the self there is a subtle combination of continuity and change. There is a sense in which what I am now is connected with the small boy looking shyly out of sixty-year-old photographs. But there is also constant change. What I do and think day by day gradually and subtly changes who and what I am. In that sense I am not the person I was sixty, fifty, forty years ago.

Therevada Buddhism developed a doctrine of *anatta* (no-self), which teaches that the self does not have an unchanging existence (and here there are echoes of a debate with Hindu traditions). Like everything else, the self is constantly changing. There are, says Buddhism, five constituents of the self, and these all change both in relation to each other and to the external world. Because of this, no *permanent* reality can be attributed to the self.[5]

The no-self doctrine is complex, and has been interpreted in various ways. A comprehensive study by Steven Collins makes careful distinctions between philosophical discussions of *anatta* and ways in which the idea functions in meditation.[6] He concludes that *anatta* 'forms part of a particular style of meditative self-analysis within the practice of

Buddhist specialists'; that is, meditation focuses on the constantly changing nature of the self. On the other hand, the doctrine enforces a careful use of language about the self which 'preserves the identity and integrity of Buddhism as an Indian system separate from Brahmanism'.[7] So there are both philosophical and practical consequences of the idea that the self constantly changes, and that therefore we cannot hold on indefinitely to the reality and permanence of our selves. In practical terms, we need to stop clinging even – perhaps especially – to the notion that in a constantly changing universe it is *we* who are the constant and abiding reality; that it is *we* who are more important than anything else. Or at its simplest and most basic, our own selfish desires and needs cannot provide a satisfactory basis for our lives. False views of the self which suppose that 'I' endures permanently are regarded as a manifestation of desire and attachment, 'and as such what is required is not so much a philosophical refutation (of such views) as a change of character in those who hold them'.[8]

This Buddhist teaching about the self is of great practical importance because it places a very strong emphasis on the need to overcome selfishness, and makes that a central issue in religion and morality. The damaging consequences of certain kinds of thinking about 'me' and 'mine' are kept before people by means of simple stories, meditation techniques and, where appropriate, by more abstract philosophical ideas. These combine to reinforce teaching of the Buddha which says that craving and selfish desires are at the heart both of our own personal problems and of major conflicts between different groups, communities and nations.[9] So the *anatta* doctrine functions as a means of discouraging selfishness, attachment, and craving; the way into liberation and peace is said to be through the extinction of selfish desires. The elimination of selfishness is central to Buddhist teaching. It would not do to gloss over the considerable differences between Christian and Buddhist views of the self

– seen, for example, in the contrast between Christian teaching about the unique value of each individual and Buddhist belief in a self which is a constantly changing flux of *khandhas*, and which in the end must be eliminated. But there is much in Buddhist teaching about overcoming selfishness which can help Christians to understand what it might mean to respond to a call to 'deny self'.

The overcoming of selfishness is at the heart of what both religions are about, however different the stories and traditions which provide their points of reference. In an old but still respected commentary, Vincent Taylor suggested an unusual interpretation of the passage in the Gospel according to Mark in which Jesus says to his disciples and others: 'Anyone who wants to be a follower of mine must renounce self . . .'[10]

Taylor pointed out that the Greek word for 'renounce' (*aparnesastho*) is translated in the *Mimes of Herodas* as 'failing to see', and so he argued that 'Let him lose sight of self' would be a legitimate and attractive translation of the words of Jesus. Self-denial, associated in Gospel passages with taking up a cross, and thereby with images of martyrdom and harsh self-abnegation, has attracted to itself in Christian imagination ideas of unpleasant and painful mortification. But substitute 'must lose sight of self' in the passage from Mark, and two possible consequences follow. One is that a hackneyed piece of Christian teaching may be seen from a different perspective; the other is that Buddhist and Christian ideas about overcoming the negative forces of the self may be seen as mutually enriching. In attempting to 'lose sight of self', Christians may well benefit from a sideways glance at Buddhist teaching.

William Johnston, whose considerable knowledge of Japanese Buddhism has provided stimulus to Christian thought, remarks upon the two ways in which the self is conceived in Zen Buddhism. On the one hand, there is the small self (*shoga*), which is also the ego or the separate self that we build up when we imagine that we are separated from God, from the universe and from other people, and this small separated self is illusory. To build it up is what traditional Christianity has called pride. We build it up when we cling to money and fame and power. Such clinging centres us on an illusory ego; it makes us forget God and destroy ourselves.

On the other hand, the big self (*taiga*)

is the self that is no longer separable but is open to the universe, to all men and women, and to God. . . . It is the same 'I' but now has this expanded consciousness which embraces all. When I lose the consciousness of separation and isolation in order to embrace the consciousness of the all, I am reaching a state that Buddhism calls emptiness and Christianity calls humility.[11]

Does this help clarify what it might mean to renounce, or deny, self? Apparently, it is not a matter of retreating into a state of pure self-abnegation; and certainly not a demand to seek some kind of martyrdom. It is, rather, a state of awareness in which we are clear-sighted and realistic about ourselves; not inflating our small egos by trying zealously to impress, manipulate or control other people, but opening ourselves to other people and to the delights and demands of the world around us. In that way we 'lose sight of self', forget about self-justification, and become better able to sympathize with others and appreciate their needs.

Losing sight of self may be encouraged by reflecting on Buddhist teaching; it also relates in interesting ways to Hindu teaching as it is found in the *Bhagavad Gita*.[12] The *Gita* accepts the common Hindu view of *karma*, that all our actions, words and thoughts have consequences which then determine the kind of people we become and the nature of our rebirth. The accumulation of *karma* is something we cannot avoid. *Karma* is usually associated with actions, and the fruits of action. Yet even if we try to be passive and do nothing, we shall build up *karma* simply by thinking. So how is it possible to avoid accumulating *karma* that will have negative effects on our future life – or lives? The answer of the *Gita* is that we can perform actions in a disinterested way, in a spirit of detachment. We perform the action, but we are not obsessed with the fruit of the action. To put it very simply, we do a good deed because it is good; because it is the right thing to do; not because we want a reward. The *Bhagavad Gita* advises us:

> Do your work [*karma*] only because it is right, and not at any time for the sake of the rewards; do not let the rewards of action be the motive, and do not be attached to inaction (B.G. 2. 47).

Bede Griffiths said of this verse:

> We must do our work, fighting the battle, doing whatever work we are required to do, but without seeking for a reward; that is, we must get rid of all egoism . . .[13]

This teaching of the *Bhagavad Gita*, in other words, expresses an important part of the Hindu method for losing sight of self in disinterested action. It appears to be in harmony with, and shed light on, those parts of the Gospels which advocate self-denial. We are to act and struggle in the world in a spirit of detachment, so that what we do is not corrupted by our own inordinate selfishness. The *Gita* advises its readers: 'Having abandoned attachment, . . . perform your work without regard to success or failure' (B.G. 2. 48).

But this is not discounting achievement, the benefits of success or the dangers of failure; rather it is advocating a way of approaching duties and responsibilities with a purity of intention, as we act out of compassion, for the sake of the deed or of another person, and not for the sake of our own reward. To use a simple illustration, when we visit someone who is ill, we do not do so in order to score a point for our own self-righteousness or reputation: 'I have visited her three times', we might say, leaving just unsaid the implication, 'and how many times have you visited her?' The visiting then becomes a competition among insecure people to bolster their own self-esteem; whether or not the visit is good for the patient becomes irrelevant. The concerned, yet disinterested, person will be as content not to visit when that is best for the patient as to visit when company is needed.

The phrase used to describe the *Gita*'s teaching about disinterested action is *nishkama karma* (action without desire). Mahatma Gandhi, who found constant inspiration in the pages of the *Bhagavad Gita*, was particularly attracted by *nishkama karma*, and made it a central part of his teaching about non-violent resistance to injustice and oppression. He was in any case convinced that renunciation is 'the highest form of religion',[14] and the *Gita*'s words about the need to perform the actions enjoined by religion in a spirit of non-attachment, without thought of reward or fear of harmful consequences, reinforced that view. In his campaigns of non-violent resistance and civil disobedience, which began in South Africa between 1894 and 1914 and came to fruition in his contributions to the independence movement in India between 1917 and 1947, Gandhi frequently referred to the need for people associated with him to act in a spirit of detachment. That meant not campaigning for independence simply for the sake of rewards or favours; and not being deterred from unpleasant and often dangerous acts by fear of brutality, imprisonment, or even death. The teaching Gandhi cherished most in the *Bhagavad Gita* was the *nishkama karma* which said, do your duty because it is your duty and do what is right because it is right. It seemed to him that the verses of the *Gita* which encouraged people to act and struggle in the daily life of the world in a spirit of detachment was of major importance for the selfless action which he regarded as essential in any attempt to establish a truly just society. It was necessary for people to lose sight of themselves if they were to make an effective contribution to the struggle for justice and freedom. Gandhi was also influenced by the New Testament, and he saw obvious connections between the call to deny oneself and take up a cross and the doctrine of *nishkama karma*. Both were concerned with the surrender of self-interest, the renunciation of rewards, and the acceptance of possible danger and injury in pursuing the goal prescribed by duty and religious belief. Like the New Testament, the *Gita* advocates an active involvement in the life of the world; but it also emphasizes the need to work and act with a true religious detachment. That does not mean being indifferent to the consequences of one's actions. It does mean being willing to lose sight of one's self in pursuit of a greater goal.

The *Bhagavad Gita* also suggests that there are beneficial personal consequences of cultivating detachment:

> The person who is in harmony, having abandoned the reward (or fruit) of action, attains final peace; the unharmonious person, driven by desire, and attached to the reward of action, is imprisoned (B.G. 5. 12).

The opening phrase is not easy to translate. Mascaro has 'this man of harmony'; Zaehner renders it as 'the integrated man'; and Chidbavananda has 'the well-poised one'.[15] The Sanskrit word they are translating is *yuktaha*, which literally means 'yoked to', 'joined', or 'united with'. The sense would be expressed precisely by the current idiom, 'the person who has got it together'. The verse is saying that people must develop a proper detachment from the rewards their actions might bring them, and do their duty for its own sake, if they are to live at peace with themselves.

In both social and personal terms, Hindu and Buddhist teaching about the need to 'lose sight of self' can add a refreshing sparkle to Christian teaching. In the rich context of Indian religious traditions, the Christian might find new and helpful ways to reflect upon the exhortations in the Gospels to 'renounce self' and 'take up his cross and follow'.[16] In New Testament readings, such words appear in contexts which focus upon the crucifixion. They may therefore give the impression that their only significance for later generations of disciples has to do either with martyrdom or with archaic ideas of blood-sacrifice: the latter, although commonplace in hymns and songs sung with gusto by many Christians, is now too bizarre to provide any help on a modern spiritual journey; the former, martyrdom, may still be a demand laid upon some who take a religious or moral commitment with absolute seriousness but will be represented only symbolically in everyday life. To supplement Christian teaching about self-denial with marginal notes taken from Hindu and Buddhist traditions may be an effective way to reinvigorate interpretations of what it might mean to 'renounce self'.

A key passage on this theme in the New Testament is Mark 8.34–7. Its importance is underlined by the fact that the same text is found in Luke 9.23–5 and Matthew 16.24–6, with a variation on the theme in John 12.24–6.[17] In Mark the passage clearly occupies a pivotal position, as his account moves from an emphasis on the public ministry of Jesus to a focus on the training of the disciples and an attempt to correct their preconceptions. Most reputable New Testament scholars regard these verses as a recollection of the original teaching of Jesus, although inevitably supplemented by warnings about the possible consequences of Christian discipleship added by a church which, by the time the words were written down, had endured persecution and thought of martyrdom as a real possibility.[18]

Mark 8.34–7 reads:

Then he called the people to him as well as his disciples and said to them, 'Anyone who wants to be a follower of mine must renounce self; he must take up his cross and follow me. Whoever wants to save his life will lose it, but whoever loses his life for my sake and for the sake of the gospel will save it. What does anyone gain by winning the wholeworld at the cost of his life? What can he give to buy his life back?'

In their original context, the words must have been chilling. The disciples were invited to 'take up a cross' if they were to follow. In later times, the cross has been domesticated. It has become an ornament, embellishing the decoration of churches and adorning individuals as pieces of jewellery. When the words were first spoken, they would have been unpleasant and unmistakable reminders of execution. Crucifixion, administered only by the Roman authorities, was common in first-century Palestine. It was also usual for those condemned to die in this hideous way to carry their cross to the place of execution. The metaphor was grim, and would have been well understood by early hearers and readers of the Gospels. For those facing the periodic outbreaks of persecution in the Roman Empire between the early sixties and the early fourth century CE, words about renouncing self and taking up a cross to follow Jesus would have had an unpleasantly realistic ring to them. Reading them as exhortations to bear extreme suffering and impending death bravely – and as promises of life 'saved' beyond the grave – would have made perfectly good sense to many of those early Christians. In particular and extreme circumstances, that may still be the case; the suffering freely undertaken by those who lay down their lives for a cause continues to excite admiration.

But there are other meanings to be drawn from such words. One way of interpreting them was for people to take themselves off to the desert, or to a monastery, and there to mortify the flesh by denying themselves the normal pleasures of life. Ascetic practices of that kind came to exert so strong a hold upon Christian imagination that in the Western Catholic Church it became natural to regard the really serious Christians as those who renounced the world, the flesh, and – with some luck and much effort – the devil, and lived lives of poverty and celibacy. The others – Christians who lived normal secular lives – could only be seen as second-class Christians, and their lapses the more excusable on that account. This way of interpreting words about self-denial created a great tradition of monasticism, which itself contributed much to Western culture. But it obscured other possible meanings of passages such as Mark chapter 8. Morna Hooker, commenting on Mark 8.34, suggests that:

> The traditional translation, 'deny himself' has been warped through being interpreted in terms of asceticism. The attitude called for is one in which self-interest and personal desires are no longer central.[19]

The words about renouncing self and taking up a cross appear to work, then, in relation to ascetics in monastic communities, hermits in their hermitages, and martyrs who are willing to lay down their lives for their beliefs. Yet if the exhortation is as limited in its applications as these categories suggest, it can hardly be regarded as a serious call to 'the people as well as his disciples'. Very few, whether because of circumstances or aptitude, are able to live the life of the monk or the martyr. The demand to overcome the worst effects of selfishness, and to subordinate self to the interests of wider communities, is a central part of Christian as well as of Indian religious traditions. But it is a part of Christian teaching that is readily overlooked. In public life contradictions between protestations and practice are clear. At the time of writing (1997) an election campaign has been fought in which neither of the main parties would risk emphasizing policies concerned more with community values than with individual self-interest, presumably because they assumed that self-interest is the primary consideration in voters' minds. It would appear to be a common judgment that in our Christian, or post-Christian, society, it really has become politically impossible to advocate the subordination of self-interest to wider social, community and international concerns. In the aftermath of the election, the new government has announced its intention of paying serious attention to ethical as well as to economic and political issues in the conduct of foreign and domestic policies. Will they be able to deliver on that? The possibility of doing so will surely be a more accurate test of Christian influence in society than is the number of converts or the size of church congregations.

A Buddhist publication for children presents the basic Buddhist teaching of the five precepts and the ten powers of goodness in a simple form that is relevant to the modern world. The five precepts, or fundamental moral commands, are reinterpreted and set out as promises:

> I promise to try not to harm any living beings.
> I promise to try not to take that which does not belong to me.
> I promise to try not to take from life more than I really need.
> I promise to try not to use my speech in harmful ways.
> I promise to try not to take harmful drinks or drugs which cloud my mind.[20]

The ten powers of goodness [*paramitas*] are explained in the following way:

1. Generosity [*dana*] – Giving, or sharing what we have with others.
2. Virtue [*sila*] – Doing good and not doing harm.
3. Unselfishness [*nekkhama*] – Giving up things which we don't need.

4. Enthusiasm/energy [*viriya*] – Putting effort into developing goodness.
5. Wisdom [*panna*] – Understanding things and people, knowing for yourself the difference between right and wrong.
6. Honesty [*sacca*] – Being truthful.
7. Determination [*adhittana*] – Being determined to do good no matter how difficult it is.
8. Patience [*khanti*] – Being patient with life.
9. Kindness [*metta*] – Being kind and helpful to all beings.
10. Even-mindedness [*upekkha*] – Being quiet inside yourself, accepting whatever happens in life calmly.[21]

Apart from the intrinsic merits of this simplified code, there are at least two other benefits. One is that it is not centred upon doctrinal or metaphysical notions, with all the attendant difficulties of such things; the other is that it reinforces ideas of considerate and unselfish conduct in a wider context than simply the personal. The promises not to harm any living beings, and not to take from life more than I really need, underlines the need to limit selfishness in relation to environmental, social, and political concerns. The list is not exceptional, and other religious and moral codes might approximate to what Buddhists are taught. But the emphasis on what is to be done, rather than on speculative systems of belief, is very positive. Christian traditions can produce examples out of their rich resources to foster attitudes of this kind. But it would be naive for Christians to assume that their own traditions have as natural or as good an historical claim to have lived gently and humbly with the world around us as have the religions of the East. Christians have come very late, and falteringly, to environmental issues. In this wider application of losing sight of self, as well as in the personal and individual sense, there is much to be learned from the less acquisitive cultures of Buddhist societies.

Christian churches do have a record of involvement in public issues, as evidenced in the British churches' calls in recent years for a fairer deal for the poor and disadvantaged, as well as a long-standing involvement in development issues, overseas aid, and medical work in many parts of the world. In South Africa and South America some churches and some Christians have been in the forefront of political battles for freedom and equality. But there is also a darker side to Christian influence in social and political activities. For all the efforts of church people to encourage reconciliation in Ireland, there can be little doubt that strongly-held Christian beliefs have reinforced ethnic and political rivalries. In the former Yugoslavia the whipping up of religious enthusiasm has been a significant factor in dividing communities. And in the USA, the alliance of Christian groups with the political right has proved to be a powerful means of generating prejudice and intolerance. Of course, other religions also have their problems. The pernicious hold of caste on Indian society was something that Gandhi, for all his good intentions, was unable to break. Hinduism still has to find ways of dealing with the prejudice against low caste people which, although declared illegal in public life, remains an important and contentious issue in India. The existence of such problems does not invalidate the claim that Christians can learn from the religious traditions of India.

In examining the light and the dark in the history of different religions it appears that it is an unthinking adherence to prescribed doctrines, an uncritical acceptance of myths as though they were facts, and a desire to promote one's own faith by castigating the faith of others that lie at the root of the negative influences of religions. The acceptance of religious teaching about caring for one's neighbours, exercising compassion, and consciously trying to overcome the worst effects of selfishness are the aspects of religions which can help to promote social as well as personal well-being.

There is a delightful and puzzling Zen Buddhist aphorism which says that 'there is not much in Buddhist teaching'. Presumably, it is suggesting that enlightenment is superior to doctrine. Is it possible for Christians to be that humble about their own traditions, I wonder? Perhaps Christians have been too concerned with purity of doctrine, and have not placed sufficient emphasis on the need to lose sight of self in practising generosity, compassion, tolerance and love.

5

Causes of Conflict or Paths to Peace?

Disinterested action is a way of expressing a personal spiritual orientation, but it is also bound up with wider moral or ethical codes. The simple Buddhist teaching quoted on pages 86–7 reflects the essential connections between religious attitudes and social ethics. Promising to try not to take from life more than I really need is to set my own needs within a context which extends from local communities to the nation and to the wider world beyond. Religious values cannot be restricted in their application simply to personal and private behaviour; if they are firmly held, they will intrude into social, commercial and political life. Yet the application of religiously-based moral convictions to public life may provoke cries of outrage from those most eager to see private lives controlled by the tenets of religious teaching. In the late nineteen-eighties Derek Worlock and David Sheppard, then respectively the Roman Catholic Archbishop and Anglican Bishop of Liverpool, wrote of their experience of trying to apply Christian ethics to public as well as private life.

> There were repeated calls to the churches to 'speak out on moral issues', and to 'give a moral lead to the nation' . . . What we were now being asked to concern ourselves with was, in effect, selective morality. The call was for the Church to condemn sexual immorality, personal laziness, violence and hooliganism. But issues of social and economic justice were not on the agenda.[1]

The fact that the moral values of religious believers have very wide application, extending throughout social and political affairs as well as applying to personal behaviour, has both positive and negative consequences. The examples of, say, Worlock and Sheppard in the Liverpool of the nineteen-eighties; of William Temple fifty years earlier; or of Martin Luther King Jr in the United States of the nineteen-sixties, are potent reminders of the ways in which religious leaders can call attention to the radical challenges presented by religious ethics to many accepted forms of social behaviour. But religious believers disagree about the interpretation of ethical codes just as they disagree about many other things. Less intelligent, or less scrupulous, leaders than those mentioned above can use religious slogans and symbols to foster hatred and violence. At a time when increasing numbers of people live in multi-faith and multi-cultural societies, religions have an important role – for good or ill – in determining attitudes to other people and expectations of how societies should be.

It is often difficult for religious believers to recognize the negative effects their beliefs may have. As a Christian minister who became a specialist in the history of religions (and therefore regarded with some suspicion by many good church people) I have been acutely aware of the tensions between the good and the bad consequences of belief. There has long been an argument between the history of religions, regarding itself as a properly empirical study which needs clear and accessible evidence to form its conclusions, and theology as a rather more speculative study concerned with belief more than with facts. Vigorous battles have been fought by history of religions specialists to escape the suffocating embrace of departments of theology (or in the old communist world, departments of Marxist studies).[2] The history of religions does not have to do with questions of whether particular beliefs are right or wrong; it is concerned to discover and analyse what it is that religious believers have

thought and done. Wandering out of the academy into a
church world is to find oneself cast in the role of an irritant,
correcting perceptions that many people would prefer to
leave unchallenged. At a popular level, sermons and
addresses in churches and by churchpeople rarely distinguish
between what is desirable, or ideal, and what is the actual
reality.

The tension becomes obvious in any discussion of whether
religion is a good or a bad thing. The exponent of a religion
(the propagandist, to use that word in its accurate and
neutral sense) will often give the impression that the religion
he is commending is good for everybody, in any situation.
The impression will be given that any person becoming a
Christian will become a better person than they would
otherwise have been. It sounds good. But when that view
is compared with observable facts, problems arise. Is
Christianity (or any other religion) always a beneficial
influence on its adherents? A strong case can be made to persuade people that it is by using attractive case-studies –
Albert Schweitzer, Mother Teresa, Martin Luther King Jr.
But think for a moment of the other side of the coin. Is Ian
Paisley better or worse, would you think, for his beliefs?
Would the Irish situation be less implacable if it were not so
bound up with belief? Would ethnic conflict in Bosnia, Serbia
and Croatia have been less likely if there had not been
connections between ethnicity and religions? John Bowker
observed that without an objective study of religions:

> it is impossible to understand the nature of so many bitter
> conflicts in the world today. For years I have been pointing
> out that religions are likely to destroy human life as we
> know it now on this planet.[3]

One area in which the good and the bad in religion are
juxtaposed, with the consequences of both clearly visible, is
that of race relations. In spite of attempts to create societies
that are religiously homogeneous, most people in the world

will of necessity have to live in multi-cultural societies. That is certainly true of people in Britain, in many parts of Europe, and in North America. Yet members of religious communities may still feel that it would be more comfortable to live in a political society that reflects one particular religious tradition, and may find it difficult to accommodate themselves to the inevitable tensions and conflicts that exist in societies in which a variety of ideologies and religious understandings compete for influence or co-exist uneasily. If we still feel the need to be convinced of the necessity for mutual understanding, sharing, and co-operation across ethnic and religious boundaries, the sorry examples of Ireland and of what used to be Yugoslavia cry out in anguish to persuade us.

In most of modern Europe, however, there is a recognition that the old orders cannot be recreated: the distant European traditions of catholic or orthodox 'Christendoms' – never entirely homogeneous, of course – have disappeared. The attempt to create a religiously homogeneous state in England in the sixteenth and seventeenth centuries had a comparative success, and the idea that to be English should also mean being Anglican still produces echoes in the national consciousness and images in the public mind on state occasions. Today we recognize that even that attempt was limited: it was never British, only English; and the gradual emancipation of Nonconformists, Catholics and Jews in the nineteenth century was part of a steady widening of access to all parts of public life which by the end of the century was also being enjoyed by Parsis, Hindus and atheists.[4] In spite of that limited progress, it is still not only possible but likely that a public figure such as the Prince of Wales will be mocked by the Press when he advocates the widening of his religious role to that of 'defender of faiths' rather than simply as titular head of the Church of England. The suggested change, far from being an example of a kind of genial looniness, is actually a sensible recognition that if the Royal Family were to continue to have a role in British life and to relate that role to religion, then the religion would have to be much wider than that represented by the Church of England.

During the last hundred years Britain has become a richly religiously-plural society, partly but by no means only as a result of immigration. In the last two decades of the nineteenth century and the first decade of the twentieth century the arrival of a limited number (perhaps 300,000) Jewish refugees from Eastern Europe provided the basis for a larger and more cosmopolitan Jewish population than the small and somewhat élite group that had lived in Britain since the seventeenth century. Those Jewish refugees encountered much prejudice during their early years in Britain, partly because their religion and culture (and for some of them for a limited period, their language) was different from that of the wider population. But they worked hard, accommodated themselves to British life, and in many cases provided models of successful adaptation to a new country. Anti-Jewishness still rears its ugly head in Britain from time to time, but for the most part being Jewish in Britain is no longer a matter to be remarked upon; it no longer divides people from one another.

The same cannot be said of those British people whose parents or grandparents arrived in this country in the late nineteen-forties and the nineteen-fifties. Paradoxically, one of the glories of the British Empire had been its multi-cultural, multi-racial and religiously-plural nature. People of all religions and many different ethnic and racial groups were equal subjects of the British Sovereign, as free to move around the Empire – if they had the means – as were their British rulers. With the birth of a new world order after the Second World War, the Empire dissolved; but people from some parts of the new Commonwealth were invited to come and work in Britain (still regarded as the 'mother country') to fill gaps in the labour market. That led to an initial immigration from the Caribbean, and subsequently from Pakistan, India, and Bangladesh; in the late nineteen-sixties and early seventies people of Indian origin arrived from East Africa. Curiously, that series of movements has come to be regarded in Britain as the essential post-1945 immigration. In fact, although not in public perception, the arrival of people from what came to be known as the 'New Commonwealth' (the 'coloured' as opposed to the 'white' Commonwealth) was only part of much wider movements of immigration and emigration. Throughout the whole period from 1945 until the nineteen-seventies (the period of primary New Commonwealth immigration) there were more white than black or coloured immigrants; more from Europe, the USA, the 'Old' Commonwealth, and especially from Ireland, than from the New Commonwealth. The term 'immigrant' has come to be applied, either in ignorance or out of malice, to the children and grandchildren of New Commonwealth immigrants, but only rarely to first-generation immigrants whose skin is white, and never to their children. That curious piece of semantics says much about racial attitudes in Britain. The other curiosity is that in discussions about immigration it is rarely acknowledged that the post-war period has been one in which more people have left the country than have entered it. We are not in danger of falling off the edge of our little island.

The arrival and settlement of people from the New Commonwealth, however, introduced into Britain religious communities which had not previously been part of the social and cultural landscape. The earliest arrivals from the Caribbean, of course, were mostly Christians, and they anticipated a warm welcome in the land that had sent missionaries to convert their ancestors to the faith. The experience of Afro-Caribbean Christians on arriving in Britain did not match their expectations. The welcome they expected was either muted or lacking altogether, and that was a great disappointment to put alongside the rejection and discrimination they suffered on racial grounds. Some Afro-Caribbean Christians persevered with the main-line churches, and today play an increasingly important role in them; others, and probably a majority, gave up in the face of the coldness of their welcome and formed the 'Black Churches' which are now a vigorous part of Christianity in urban Britain. Other newcomers, from the Indian sub-continent, brought with them religious faiths and practices which had previously been encountered only occasionally and among very small groups in the UK. Today the mosques, temples and gurdwaras of Muslims, Hindus, Jains and Sikhs provide a colourful, fascinating and spiritually exciting part of Britain's religious tapestry. In addition to some 300,000 Jews, there are now more than a million Muslims, about 400,000 Hindus, perhaps 300,000 Sikhs, and 30,000 Jains in Britain.[5] In all of these faith communities the proportion of British-born members steadily increases in relation to the first-generation immigrants (in many cases now quite elderly), so that although links with the old countries of origin remain important for some, it is also important that Christians should think of Muslims, Hindus, Sikhs, and Jains not as exotic but short-lived plants blossoming in the wilderness of urban Britain, but as permanent additions to the stock of British religious life.

Christian attitudes to people of other faiths in Britain are sometimes positive. Christians are usually well-represented in local inter-faith groups. And there is a slowly-growing recognition of the importance of an understanding and awareness of other faiths in such areas as religious education.[6] But far too many Christians are dismissive of other faiths, assuming that they are simply 'wrong'. It is difficult to take that view of other people's beliefs and at the same time to respect them and acknowledge their place in the life of the nation. The theological denigration of the beliefs of other people can too readily be harnessed to racial prejudice, so that minority ethnic groups come to be viewed as a threat to a supposedly cohesive national life and at the same time as dangerously misguided in belief.

In spite of the benign intentions of Christian people, Christian beliefs can all too easily lead to negative views of other faith communities. The best intentions of fervent believers only rarely lead to tolerance and a willing acceptance of those who differ from them. Yet in a religiously plural and ethnically mixed society, the consequences of deeply held beliefs which are intrinsically hostile to the beliefs of other people are likely to be extremely damaging. The fact that people of other faiths are now represented by significant numbers and well-established communities in Britain poses questions about how positive – or negative – the social impact of Christian belief is. One of the great challenges posed to Christians by other faith communities in Britain today is a challenge to the tolerance, the depth of understanding, and the essential decency of Christian people. Christians somehow have to learn to purge their evangelism of dismissive or arrogant attitudes towards those who differ from them in matters of belief.

As a start to this difficult process, it might be helpful to reflect on the ninth commandment. 'Do not give false evidence against your neighbour', we presume, was originally a warning against faking evidence in hearings which dealt with accusations within a relatively small and homogeneous community. But part of a modern interpretation of the commandment may well be to resist the temptation to misrepresent the faith – or the consequences of the faith – of other people. This modest aim requires not only a good deal of knowledge of what it is that people believe and practice, but also a level of sympathetic understanding not always found among those who rejoice in their own belief in a God of love. Attempts to understand necessarily involve actually getting to know members of other faith communities, seeing how they live, and visiting their places of worship. It will be helped by learning something about their traditions, perhaps reading a selection of their scriptures. I mentioned in the first chapter how important it seemed to my Hindu friends in

Vellore that I was making the attempt to learn some Sanskrit in order to enter into serious discussions about their traditions. Whilst the opportunity to do that will come to only a few people, it does demonstrate the value of taking trouble to understand other people's faith at some depth, and the very great – I think disproportionate – feelings of gratitude, friendship and appreciation engendered by doing so.

In a religiously diverse society, in which ethnic and racial differences are exaggerated, terms such as 'immigrant' widely misused, and the history of the dependence of Britain upon its colonial empire almost entirely ignored, Christians have an important role to play in fostering harmony between people of different racial and religious backgrounds. But they will only do it by reassessing their evangelistic activities, and deliberately incorporating education about other faiths and attitudes of tolerance into their programmes. Competition between different faith groups should be about who can be the most tolerant, not about whose faith is held to be the most true.

Inter-racial and inter-ethnic conflicts are very damaging to the cohesion of modern societies, as well as to the personal well-being of their members. Even worse consequences follow when rivalries lead to outright conflict. Religions play their part, for good or ill, in many wars, in civil wars and in the vicious hatred of ethnic cleansing. Georges Khodr once claimed that 'All wars are metaphysical; one can only go to war religiously.'[7]

It is clear that a kind of religious zeal can feed the emotions required to garner enthusiasm for an all-out war. The appeal to high principle, to fighting for a great cause, is one which is frequently heard when war looms, but one which should always be resisted by the discerning citizen. Wars fought for principles are almost always worse than wars fought for limited ends, as Herbert Butterfield astutely acknowledged.[8] But in the modern world it is not only the appeal to a kind of religious zeal that is used to foster animosity against others, but also the actual presence of religions, playing their own roles in encouraging and justifying war between people of different faiths. A recent World Council of Churches' publication begins with a reference to the apparent paradox of Christian intentions and political realities.

> Almost all Christians would agree immediately that reconciliation and peacemaking are part of the Christian calling, both for churches and Christian organizations and for Christian individuals. That the churches and Christian people have failed in their efforts almost entirely is all too evident. That Christian people and even Christian beliefs and practices have been a contributing presence in many circumstances of violent conflict is a painful truth that we must face.[9]

Yet all the major religions have developed teaching about the prevention of war and the pursuit of peace, and from them all it is possible to draw illustrations of believers who have made considerable sacrifices to maintain a witness for peace. In the twentieth century there has been a fascinating process of inter-faith co-operation and learning, as peace-makers have drawn on religious traditions other than their own to enhance their understanding and their practices. I have written elsewhere of the delight of Mahatma Gandhi when first he read the Sermon on the Mount, and of ways in which Martin Luther King Jr looked to Gandhi's practice of non-violent resistance to provide the method for his own Christian leadership of the civil rights movement in the USA.[10] Gandhi first read the Sermon on the Mount when he was a law student in England in the late eighteen-eighties. Having been advised to read the Bible, but having had no help in going about the task, Gandhi started at the beginning and read through it as one might with any book. Gandhi confessed his lack of enthusiasm for the Book of Numbers, and one can imagine the tedium the early part of the exercise must have induced. But he arrived at the New Testament, and very soon after that at Matthew chapter five, and the Sermon on the Mount. Here, he thought, was something much more exciting. Gandhi said of Matthew's presentation of the teaching of Jesus in the Sermon on the Mount that it

> went straight to my heart. I compared it with the *Gita*. The verses, 'But I say unto you, that ye resist not evil: but whosoever shall smite thee on thy right cheek, turn to him the other also. And if any man take away thy coat let him have thy cloak too' delighted me beyond measure . . . My young mind tried to unify the teaching of the *Gita*, *The Light of Asia*, and the Sermon on the Mount. That renunciation was the highest form of religion appealed to me greatly.[11]

Gandhi's belief in the value of renunciation was partly the result of Jain influence on his life at home and on his native area of Gujarat. He integrated that quite naturally into his own Hindu faith, and related it to Hindu ascetic practices. The practice of renunciation became especially important in Gandhi's personal life from the the time he and his family began to live in his first ashram, in South Africa in 1906. But it was more especially in the development of his theories and practices of non-violent resistance, which he called *satyagraha*, or the struggle for truth, that his subtle mixing of ideas from Hindu, Buddhist, Jain and Christian traditions was woven into the marvellous tapestry of a profoundly moral and religious life. His non-violence was related not only to issues of civil rights in South Africa and the struggle for independence in India, but also to actual situations of war and peace, in the Boer War and the Zulu rebellion in South Africa and in the rather mixed attitudes he took to the First and Second World Wars.[12] His constant search for means to outwit the British Raj, and to oppose superior force by tactics that would present the rulers of India with difficult and sometimes embarrassing choices, was consistent with what appear to be the intentions of the Sermon on the Mount.

To most readers, the Sermon on the Mount seems to be hopelessly impractical. Why should the sorrowful be 'blessed'? And is it not ludicrous to imagine that the meek, or gentle, shall inherit the earth? It was Mark Twain, reporting on the Golden Jubilee celebrations of Queen Victoria, whose delicious irony put together the display of military might and professions of Victorian morality and religiosity in a head-line, 'Blessed are the meek, for they shall inherit the earth'. It does seem unlikely. And what is one to make of turning the other cheek, or volunteering an extra mile when pressed into service to carry a conqueror's pack for one mile?

A recent exposition offers refreshing insights into these obscure verses, and shows how they can be interpreted in a Gandhian sense. Walter Wink suggests, for example, that in using the verb *antistenai* for 'resist' in 'Do not resist those who wrong you' (Matt. 5.39), the gospel is actually urging the prohibition of lethal violence. He points out that the Greek word is often used as a military term, suggesting not just resistance, but standing against somebody in battle.[13] So the text in Matthew should be read as a warning against violent resistance, saying in effect:

> do not be supine or complicit in your oppression; but on the other hand, do not react violently to it either. Rather, find a third way, a way that is neither submission nor assault, neither fight nor flight.[14]

Similarly, Wink argues that turning the other cheek is advocated as a response to a contemptuous backhanded slap on the *right* cheek administered by a right handed person. A serious blow intended to disable would land on the *left* cheek. That is what is invited in response to the slap which indicates the recipient's servility. 'All right, then, hit me properly, if that is what you want to do', the powerless person replies, turning the left cheek to receive a serious blow. But that is not what is intended. The assailant is left unsure about what to do next. 'If someone in authority presses you into service for one mile, go with him two,' says the next verse in Matthew. The soldier, with power to impress a conquered person to carry his baggage for one mile, might be seriously compromised by insistence to go a further mile – against the rules under which the soldier operated. Again, the powerless respond in ways that are appropriate to their own situation, using ridicule and humour in the absence of other weapons of defence. The lesson is not: 'never resist, do not stand up for rights'. It is, rather: 'resist in whatever way is available to you, and appropriate to your situation'.

That was the kind of technique used by Gandhi, who in 1930 launched perhaps his most effective demonstration in the Salt Tax Satyagraha. The action drew attention to the way in which an expensive foreign administration was maintained at least in part by levying taxes on items essential to a poverty-ridden population. Gandhi organized a march from his ashram in Ahmedabad to Dandi, 240 miles away by the sea. As he and his supporters walked, they attracted more and more followers. The national press carried the story. Reporters from other countries joined the marchers, and international attention focused on their cause. When they eventually arrived at the coast, the marchers distilled salt from the sea water in a crude fashion. It provided little salt, but theoretically it broke the law which said that salt could only be had after payment of a tax. What were the authorities to do? If they arrested the marchers (as they did in the end), they would look ridiculous; if they did not, they would condone the breaking of the law. It was a classic piece of non-violent resistance, in the spirit of the Sermon on the Mount.

Undoubtedly, the crossing of traditional lines of demarcation between religions enabled peace-seekers to discover new ways of expressing their concerns, and provided them with new methods of campaigning for peace.[15] Gandhi's influence was of seminal importance, quite independently of its actual political success or failure in the Indian nationalist movement. Peter Calvocoressi was surely right in suggesting of Gandhi that:

> He became a symbol. His career led millions to believe that big problems may be settled without violence, so that he has a lasting place in the history of ideas as well as in the history of India.[16]

Gandhi's ideas were only effectively translated into Western and Christian contexts after the Second World War. The most notable interpreter of Gandhian methods (although not, of course, ideology) in the West was Martin Luther King Jr. The uses he made of techniques of non-violent resistance, non-co-operation, and civil disobedience, are well known. The civil rights movement in the USA in the nineteen-sixties spread an awareness of the possible effectiveness of Gandhian techniques in a Western, and indeed, Christian context. By that time, connections between Gandhian-style non-violent tactics and broader concerns of the peace movements were already being made. In 1958 the World Council of Churches published a Provisional Study Document on 'Christians and the Prevention of War in an Atomic Age – A Theological Discussion'. The document was studied at a consultation arranged by the National Christian Council of India in conjunction with the Fellowship of Reconciliation and the Christian Institute for the Study of Religion and Society, and held at Nagpur in 1959. The advantages of subjecting such documents (at that time inevitably displaying a North American/European emphasis) to a wider international and inter-cultural critique were evident in the report, which among other things said:

> . . . traditional methods (of resolving international con-

flicts) have always had war as ultimate sanction. What we need today are alternative methods which will be effective without this sanction. In our struggle for national freedom in India non-violent resistance or *satyagraha* was indeed used with success. There may have been several unique factors which made it effective in that particular instance. The techniques of non-violent resistance are as yet in their beginnings. It is also misunderstood and abused by many in political life within India. It is extremely important that they be developed in international relations on responsible lines . . . Christians have a special responsibility in this matter.[17]

Europeans and North Americans, therefore, had the opportunity to benefit from a wider cultural perspective, and a better understanding of Gandhian *satyagraha*, than had been commonly available in their countries. Indeed, it was in relation to the threatened use of nuclear weapons that Gandhian-style tactics of non-violence and civil disobedience were readily adopted by Christian and other protestors in the West. By the early nineteen-eighties a fascinating mix of cultural and religious values was contributing to campaigns against the use of nuclear weapons. It is estimated that in the autumn of 1981 there were two million peace demonstrators across Europe, and most of them were marching and demonstrating in the style and with at least some of the ideas of Gandhi. At the same time, Buddhist influences were being felt, and Eastern and Western ideas and techniques were mixing together. When attempts were made to evict demonstrators from Greenham Common on the 14 May 1983, Buddhist monks from the Milton Keynes Japanese Buddhist Centre joined the Greenham women in a noisy protest which on that occasion included the beating of Buddhist drums. Added to the cultural mix were some of the rather inchoate ideas of the New Age movements. One of the gates at Greenham Common was renamed the 'New Age Gate' by campaigners, and some defendants in court in nearby Newbury insisted on taking the oath in the name of the Goddess.

For Christians, however, the most usual basis for thinking about issues of war and peace remained that of the Just War doctrine. Originating in Greek thought, and refined by St Augustine in the fifth century and by other theologians later, the ideas of the Just War have provided rules to limit the worst effects of war, many of which have passed into international law. The doctrine sets out conditions to be applied when a state is considering whether or not to go to war (*ius ad bellum*). These include provisions that:

> war should not be declared until every means to avert it have been exhausted;
> there should be a proper declaration of war by a legitimate authority;
> there should be 'moral certainty' that the just cause (usually the defence of a piece of territory) should be victorious (and so one should not risk lives by fighting a losing battle for the sake of principle);
> and there should be a careful weighing of the 'proportionality' between the good to be achieved by victory and the evil that will inevitably occur in war.

A separate set of rules (*ius in bello*), some of them now part of the Geneva Convention, stipulate conditions that should be observed once a war has broken out. These include respecting the rights of neutrals, and not deliberately attacking civilian populations.

In practice, of course, many of these rules are broken time and time again. Yet that seems no more a reason to ignore them than it would be to rescind laws against murder and robbery on the grounds that quite a lot of people break them. And in so far as these rules have become incorporated into international law, they provide a possible means of bringing war criminals to book when a conflict has ended.

Not surprisingly, other great religious traditions have also developed guidance or rules about war and peace. There is a common perception, fed now by images of a resurgent Islam emerging from a long period of colonial subjugation, that Islam is an especially warlike religion. Islam's astonishingly rapid spread around the Mediterranean in its first hundred years was largely the result of conquest, although we should remember that many of the conquered people lived under corrupt governments and may well have regarded the coming of Islam as a liberation. Muhammad's own early struggles against the rulers of Mecca involved a number of battles, and in the course of that early development there arose the doctrine of *jihad*. *Jihad* is not synonymous with warfare – in Arabic the actual word for warfare is *harb*, and war in general is also described as *qital* (killing) – but suggests rather a struggle for the furthering of the religion and morality of Islam and opposition to anti-Islamic influences. Among Muslims there also developed principles about how wars should be conducted, although Muslims share with Christians the tendency not to live up to the ideals enunciated in their scriptures and traditions. Islamic rules stipulate that wars should not be undertaken for purely aggressive purposes, and that no more force than necessary should be used. War in defence of territory or against a tyrant is regarded as legitimate. Conversion at the point of the sword is forbidden, as are attacks on non-combatants. Muslim soldiers were also instructed to respect the environment, for example by sparing fruit trees and protecting wells during warfare, and to care for prisoners. A description of peace by a contemporary Muslim may help give a positive impression of Islamic thinking about war and peace. Giving the Sydney Bailey Memorial Lecture at Westminster Abbey in March, 1997, Crown Prince Hassan bin Tala of Jordan said:

Peace is the opposite of war, is it not? On this view, in the absence of war, there must be peace. But this is a shallow

definition which does little to advance our understanding.
I think of my own region, the Middle East. For the last
half-century between relatively brief outbreaks of war, my
region has existed in an uneasy, shadowy state. Tension
and hostility were ever-present. This was not a state of
war, but by no means could it be described as a state of
peace. Perhaps we would do better, then, to define peace in
a positive way. On this view, peace means the presence of
justice. It means mutual respect; it means compassion and
humility, tolerance and empathy. A recent survey found
that the sense of humiliation was a principal cause of the
Palestinian *intifada*. Wherever our sense of human dignity
is affronted, there can be no true peace. Peace therefore
means acknowledging that others have a valid viewpoint,
and a self-validating sense of history, and a pain within
their souls as great as their own.[18]

Those fine sentiments would do credit to the follower of
any religion, attempting to convert into the hard currency of
international diplomacy the concern and respect for others
which is bound up with the ethical teaching of most great
religions.

It is a common perception of Buddhism that its followers
are exceptionally endowed with peaceful virtues. In the wake
of the Second World War, Buddhist missionary movements
from South East Asia and Japan emphasized the peaceful
nature of Buddhism as part of their appeal to Western
Europe. It is true that early Buddhism spread through the
preaching and teaching of its *bhikkhus*, and not by conquest;
and that the personal ethics of Buddhism encourage peaceful
pursuits in teaching on 'right livelihood'. A text says of the
duties of lay people that there are

certain trades and pursuits which the householder should
not follow since these are not in accord with the precepts;
these are enumerated as: trade in weapons, trade in human
beings, in flesh, intoxicants, and trade in poison.[19]

But there seems to be no less difficulty in Buddhism than in Christianity in translating the ideal ethic for the individual into a comprehensive and feasible ethic for nations. It has not followed as a matter of course that international relations have been more peaceful where Buddhist institutions and ideas have had a recognizable influence on public life.[20] In spite of the important place given to *ahimsa* in Buddhism as abstention from the taking of life, attitudes to the conduct of war seem to have been similar to those found historically among Christians and Muslims. Saddhatissa records the Buddha's advice to King Ajatesathu, when asked whether a proposed military attack would be successful. The Buddha's concerns were that women and girls should not be detained by force, that *arahants* (strivers after enlightenment) should be protected, and that the shrines of the conquered people should not be dishonoured. So the practical consequences of Buddhist ideas seem to have been that warfare is something that happens, however regrettable it might be; that serious seekers after enlightenment should be exempt from war; and that rules (bearing some relationship to parts of the *ius in bello* rules of the Just War) should be observed. While the serious Buddhist pursued enlightenment, the ordinary affairs of life, including conflict and war, would continue, but should be mitigated by humanitarian concerns.

Buddhism, like other religions, is influenced by its social and political contexts. During the last fifty years Buddhists have been among those few people to have actually suffered the devastation caused by the dropping of atomic bombs, and the scars of that experience have served as a reminder of the horrors of war. Buddhist involvement in peace movements around the world has often focused particularly on nuclear disarmament. In the same period the world has watched with some admiration, but not a hint of intervention, the way in which the peaceful Buddhists of Tibet have been crushed and forced into exile by the Chinese. The Dalai Lama has presented the cause of his subjugated people with dignity and humour. He has attracted great attention in the media, and at public meetings, and is one of the most respected spiritual leaders of the time. His message contains the assumption that the conquest of people's minds and hearts is in the end more important than the conquest of territory, and that the enduring triumphs are of mind and spirit, not of military might. In the West, Buddhists – especially Japanese Buddhists – have built their peace pagodas and marched in demonstrations against nuclear weapons. In all these ways, modern Buddhists have attempted to extend the doctrine of individual *ahimsa* into a set of ideas which might influence national and international policies.

Clearly, the great religious traditions all have much to learn about how to avoid being used as symbols of separation and hostility. But they also have much in common, as well as something to teach one another, when it comes to enunciating policies for peace. In the best of the traditions there can be found an emphasis on peace and reconciliation, an insistence on connections between peace and justice, and a desire to see the 'rules' about the conduct of war and the resolution of conflicts incorporated into international law.

Another matter of increasing social and political concern is the environment. As people become increasingly aware of the possibly calamitous consequences of using up non-renewable natural resources, of damaging the ozone layer, and of spoiling much of the home which is our dwelling and our delight, so religious thinkers increasingly ask what their traditions have to say about the environment. In discussions that follow from this, we must beware of swallowing too readily the claims for environmental purity which theologians in their ingenuity discover in their texts, whilst at the same time welcoming any positive re-assessments which help religions to be allies in a critically important cause. It is undoubtedly through the work of scientists and their allies that an awareness of the problems and of ways of overcoming them most often arise. But religions help to shape attitudes and form values, and they have their part to play. In asking what that part may be, we are most likely to make progress if we look at religious traditions of other people as well as at our own.

The association of Christianity and Christians with colonialism, industrial development, and technological advance – all three of which are related to each other – tends to cast serious and not entirely undeserved doubts on the Christian record on the environment. Industrialization is profligate with natural resources. The fact that the rapid development of industrialization in the West was dependent upon sources of raw materials and large captive markets in colonial territories is one reason why the process of industrial development began in the West, and was only much later transferred to other parts of the world. That development both fed upon and was maintained by the possession of large territories of subjugated peoples, and their resources. But were there other, and more clearly ideological, reasons for the initial development of modern industries in the West?

Before people became so aware of the environmental problems generated by industrial growth, it was sometimes claimed that the West's leading role in the process was the result of a biblical view of history and development, and of human responsibility for everything on the earth. In a book first published in 1964, a Dutch theologian, Arend Th. van Leeuwen, wrote:

> The modern technological revolution is . . . the outcome of a unique course of civilization in the West, in which clearly discernible spiritual motives and a particular view of God, man and the world have played a decisive part.[21]

A linear view of history, and with it the expectation of continuing progress, led not only to the modern technological revolution but also to expectations of continual economic advance, with consequences not then foreseen.

More recent Christian thinking has taken account of

environmental issues, and is now inclined to emphasize different – but equally biblical – ideas. These include the belief that the world is the result of God's creative activity, and not merely accidental; that it is flawed but renewable; and that people are the agents of God in that renewal. Environmentally friendly ideas are certainly present in Christian liturgies – for example, in the Benedicite, or Song of Creation, included in the Anglican form of Morning Prayer and expressing a delight in the natural world:

Bless the Lord all created things
sing his praise and exalt him for ever.
. . . bless the Lord, all rain and dew . . . all winds that blow
. . . light and darkness . . . frost and cold . . .
. . . mountains and hills . . . seas and rivers . . .
sing his praise and exalt him for ever.[22]

Concern about the relationship between humans and nature has also encouraged a fresh look at the oldest Christian tradition in Britain – Celtic Christianity. Long before the arrival of St Augustine from Rome in 597 CE, there had been native Christians in Britain. There were probably some small Christian communities in the second century, and there are many references to a Celtic church in the fourth century.[23] The Celtic church, probably made up of small rural communities rather than of sophisticated town-dwellers, appears to have incorporated earlier religious interest in nature into its Christianity. The sense Celtic Christianity had that the natural world is good and that God may be found in creation, is reflected in some words of St Patrick, one of the great figures of the Celtic church who died around 460:

God of heaven and earth, seas and rivers,
God of sun and moon, of all the stars,
God of high mountain and lowly valleys . . .
He has a dwelling in heaven and earth and sea
and in all things that are in them.[24]

One of the differences between the Semitic religions – Judaism, Christianity and Islam – and the religions of India is represented by the cyclical view of life commonly found in India. Birth leads to death, which leads to rebirth, and so on. A similar view is held of the cosmos. Hinduism conceives of vast aeons of time during which the universe comes into being, exists, eventually declines, and dies. But that death, too, is followed by another birth, a new creation, and life begins again. Belief in rebirth, which still seems to be held strongly by large numbers of people in India, allows the possibility of a human being reborn in animal form. This, it is claimed, creates a feeling of greater harmony between different life-forms. Allied to this is a reverence for life, strongly represented among Jains but also part of many Hindu traditions. Those who practise reverence for life will consciously avoid killing or injuring any living creature, and this influences behaviour along a broad spectrum, from Gandhian non-violence in political contexts to not killing insects with which one has to share the immediate environment. Far from holding ideas about subduing and controlling the natural world, traditional Hindu beliefs have had much more to do with living as part of the world of nature, and this may suggest that care for the environment is more natural to Hindu than to Christian systems of belief. It was the claim of Rabindranath Tagore that:

> Indian civilisation has been distinctive in locating the source of regeneration, material and intellectual, in the forest, not in the city. India's best ideas have come where man was in communion with trees and rivers and lakes, away from crowds. . . The culture that has arisen from the forest has been influenced by the diverse processes of renewal of life which are always at play in the forest, varying from species to species, from season to season, in sight and sound and smell.[25]

Hindus also seem to have an innate respect for those who, on religious grounds, live simply and consume little. Although very few renounce virtually all possessions on the model of the *sannyasi*, there remains an expectation that someone who is to be regarded as a holy man or woman, or who effects to teach religion to others, should live a life in which material needs are kept to a minimum. This is one reason why the foreign missionary in India, although respected for contributions to education and medical work, has always been an ambiguous and slightly curious figure in religious terms. The Westerner, however modest his lifestyle may be by European or American standards, will inevitably appear to be rich and to be a conspicuous consumer of goods and services in the eyes of the Indian villager. That is perhaps one reason why the rare European who manages to live like a Hindu *sannyasi* – and Bede Griffiths is the example I have already mentioned – is so much admired. The lifestyle clothes the religious message with an authenticity it will otherwise lack.

Buddhism may also appear to be a religion which would naturally be environmentally friendly. Curiously, this is not necessarily the case. Ian Harris, writing on Buddhism in *Attitudes to Nature*, said of the claim that Buddhism is more positive than Christianity in its concern for the natural world: 'I find this attitude difficult to square with any actually occurring Buddhist tradition and shall argue that the Christian situation is more or less precisely mirrored in Buddhism.'[26]

This, Harris argues, is because of the view of early Buddhism that all conditioned things are inherently unsatisfactory, and that as a consequence 'the world is endless, meaningless and purposeless'.[27]

Against this, he points out that belief in rebirth encourages a sense of fellow feeling with other humans and other creatures, and that essential to Buddhist teaching is the very strong stress it places on loving-kindness and compassion to

all beings. He concludes that, almost in spite of the purity of
its original teaching, Buddhism has come to emphasize a
spirit of toleration and co-operation with the natural world.
But we should also note that reverence for life, living in
harmony with the natural world, and living simply are all
consistent with Buddhist teaching and lifestyles.

Modern Buddhists clearly do make frequent connections
between their beliefs, and attitudes which promote non-
exploitative living in relation both to the environment and
other people. The list of promises asked of Buddhist children
(page 86) includes a simple reference to *ahimsa* ('I promise to
try not to harm any living beings'), and to limiting demands
on resources ('I promise to try not to take more from life than
I really need'). A document on Buddhist education includes a
statement which reflects strong desire to relate Buddhist
teaching and environmental concerns:

> On many fundamental issues Buddhism presents a
> challenge to the secular world. It challenges its emphasis
> on egoistic self-interest, material gain, power and fame; its
> short-sightedness in seeking merely the rewards of this
> brief span of life; its failure to appreciate the fundamental
> inter-connectedness of all living organisms and systems; its
> exploitation of non-human forms of life; and, above all, its
> loss – even denial – of spiritual insights and values.[28]

The encouraging aspect of discussions about religion and
the environment is the discovery of how keenly the need to
protect our natural heritage is being promoted in many
different religious traditions. In spite of differences between
belief systems, there does seem to be increasing agreement
about the need to live simply, not to consume more than we
need, and to cherish the beauty and wonder of the world
we inhabit. Some words from an ancient Indian source,
commonly used to conclude ceremonies and prayers, express
the sense of peace (*shanti*) that reflection on the world
around can bring:

Peace of sky, peace of earth,
peace of waters, peace of plants.
Peace of trees, peace of all gods, peace of *Brahman*,
peace of the universe, peace of peace,
May that peace come to me.[29]

6

Following the Path

Faith is like a journey. Many religious believers appear to
be looking for security, for something constant to cling
to in a rapidly changing world. And religions offer the solace
of ancient traditions and familiar rituals. Yet to embrace a
religious faith is to risk the unpredictability often found
when travelling: a sudden perception of something totally
unfamiliar in the landscape; a panicky feeling of loss of
control when people don't understand you; an odd feeling in
the stomach which is perhaps part of the excitement and, in
retrospect only, part of the pleasure of exploring new territory. Alas, whether in journeys or religion, there are plenty of
people who cannot tolerate difference. For them, travelling
abroad needs to be fortified by fish and chips and beer, and
loud English voices. For many people, too, religious activity
has to feel like some familiar other – a pop concert, the now
long-lost music hall, half-forgotten family gatherings with
parlour games and feigned camaraderie. It would be churlish
to be too critical of that need of the familiar and the reassuring. Equally, it would be misguided to ignore the needs of
those who want to make progress, whether in travel or
religion, by exploring something new, crossing cultural
boundaries, waking up to new ideas. Those who, in short, are
willing to take risks in order to make progress.

Can there be a Christianity for the risk-takers? As
Christians prepare to celebrate the millennium and nearly
2,000 years of dating the calendar from the time of Christ, it
seems to many on the fringes of faith that much of what

today is expressed as Christian is simply an embarrassment. How are we to discover alternatives? I have suggested that some of the comments from other faiths written on the flyleaf during my own journey have helped to map out a path of discovery that can be travelled with integrity. The hope of this book is that others will also feel encouragement in some of the insights gleaned from those of other faiths, and doing so will rediscover a more profound and challenging Christian faith for the twenty-first century.

Part of the genius of Indian religion seems to me to be its inclusiveness and comprehensiveness in belief and practice. Of course, all religions have their dark edges of intolerance, and the traditions which grew up in India are no exception. There are narrowly nationalistic parties in modern India capitalizing on the appeal of religion. Yet in spite of the seductive nature of such politics, India has hung on to the original intention of its constitution and remains a secular state, in which all religions have legal equality. And in spite of the obvious intolerances of Hindu history – seen especially in the system of caste, and the exclusion of very low caste people from religious and social privileges – open and tolerant views of divergent beliefs and spiritual practices have been contained under the capacious umbrella of Hinduism.

The most accessible of Hindu scriptures is the *Bhagavad Gita*, first translated into English in 1785 and widely available in the West.[1] Part of the interest of the text is that the *Gita* sets out three ways in which spiritual progress may be made. One is the path of wisdom, or intellectual understanding (*jnana*), which in Hindu teaching also incorporates an appropriate knowledge of rituals; another is the path of action (*karma*), which in modern terms might be seen as a Gandhian, or social action, approach to Hinduism; and the third is the way of loving devotion (*bhakti*), which is concerned with devotion to God, and so also with popular worship, chanting and singing. Some commentators see these three as alternative paths, others as complementary. Certainly, they enshrine in the *Gita* a recognition that different people have different religious needs, and different things to contribute to the working out of a tradition.

The three paths of the *Gita*, it seems to me, are of interest well beyond the Hindu communities in which the text is most commonly read. The ways of knowledge and intellectual understanding, social action, and devotional religion appear in all the major religious traditions, even though they are not given the names used in the *Gita*. In these post-ecumenical times it may be especially helpful for Christians to reflect on the significance of those three approaches. For the most important divisions between Christians now are marked, not by denominations, but by different approaches to Christian faith and life. Many Christians place great emphasis upon emotional experience, whether in explicitly charismatic groups or in worship described by its detractors as 'happy-clappy'. Others preach a gospel of social action in which the touchstone of authenticity is a 'bias towards the poor'. And others (a beleaguered minority, I fear) struggle with the difficult intellectual questions facing people who profess a religious faith today and wish that within the churches more attention could be paid to such matters. It is not impossible (although it is somewhat unlikely) that all three may come together. What is more likely is that different Christian communities will need to provide for different needs, and to consciously opt for one of the possible 'paths'. The recognition that we are not all the same because we profess more or less the same religious faith is essential. The pressure put upon people in some Christian communities to conform to a supposedly orthodox norm, to become pale copies of mediocre role models, is intolerable.

So how are we to explore something new, cross cultural boundaries, and wake up to fresh ideas? The first step may be to recognize the provisional nature of all religious – including Christian – ideas. We are told – probably rightly – that many people can only make something of religion if religious ideas are expressed in simplistic terms. The simple worshipper, it is assumed, needs certainty. He or she must not be confused by doubts that may be cast upon their beliefs. And so supposed events that none of us ever experience or could have actual knowledge of – miracles, people dying and coming to life again, virgins giving birth, the world being created in seven days – are left without interpretation, their mythological nature only penetrated by individuals struggling with their private doubts. The questions of how the not-so-simple are to be provided for, or the simple worshipper encouraged to make progress towards more subtle ideas, are left unanswered.

In chapter 2 much was made of the apophatic tradition, the teaching found in many Christian sources as well as in Hinduism, Buddhism and even Islam that God is greater than any of our conceptions of him. Whatever we say of God, he is always more or other than our descriptions and our ideas. We cannot domesticate the transcendent reality to which religious believers give the name 'God'. Such ideas have played an important part in the writing of many Christian theologians, and are indispensable to the intellectual traditions of Buddhism and Hinduism. If the journey of faith made by an increasing number of Westerners takes them in the direction of Buddhism and Vedanta it may well be because only so can they escape what appear to be the impossible simplicities of so much Christian teaching. Those of us who find apophatic ideas helpful have to be bold enough to express our thoughts even in Christian circles. The ideas, after all, *are* Christian, even if some of us only discover them after a circuitous journey to the East.

An example from modern Hindu history may be helpful here. Vivekananda, a great figure in the renewal of Hinduism in the nineteenth century, was a student in Calcutta when he was attracted by the great Hindu saint, Ramakrishna.[2] He was impressed by the simplicity and obvious spirituality of the Bengali mystic, and he became one of his closest disciples. Ramakrishna was essentially a *bhakti*, a fervent worshipper of the goddess *Kali*, whom he called Mother, although his Hinduism was eclectic and embraced a number of not altogether consistent traditions. Ramakrishna, from a simple village background and with hardly any formal education, had the good sense to recognize in the young Narendra a person of considerable intellectual ability, and he encouraged Narendra to pay particular attention to the philosophy of *advaita Vedanta*. Somewhat like monism in Western philosophy, *advaita* (the word means 'not dual') teaches that the world and everything in it is to be properly understood as one great interrelated whole. Our sense experience conveys to us a world full of different and often apparently contradictory things; but were we able to see things as they really are, we should recognize that there is only one reality to which everything in the world relates, of which everything is part. This is not the place to explore the ideas of *advaita*.[3] But it is worth pointing out that by commending *advaita* to the young Narendra, Ramakrishna recognized the need of a different approach from his own *bhakti* if a more intellectual person were also to make progress. When Narendra Nath became Vivekananda, he made *advaita* the centre of his own religious teaching, and was particularly successful in commending this approach in the West. He acknowledged the need many people have for pictures of God or the gods to which they can relate; but he was always keen to encourage people to move on, with the opportunity of following a path on which there were signposts to intellectual progress. The earlier stages should lead on to more profound understanding, he suggested; '. . . the Indian Vedantist does not curse the preceding steps; he looks back and blesses them, and he knows that they were true, only wrongly perceived.'[4]

The paradox is that the Westerners who discovered in the Ramakrishna Mission an antidote to what they regarded as the crude ideas of Christianity did not know what surprisingly similar thoughts had occurred to Christian theologians. Mention has already been made of a line of thought, from Dionysius and Aquinas and on to Tillich in the twentieth century, which would have appealed to the Western Vedantists.[5] But many of them seem to have assumed that such ideas could only be found in the East. In tracing a line of thought through Christian teaching, Raimundo Panikkar reminds us that

God is always absent. Any presence of God is . . . a veil, a manifestation, and thereby a disfiguring, or at best a figuring. A God who is not absent will be a simple idol. *Resurrexit, non est hic!* (He is not here. He is risen. Matt. 28.6).[6]

Many Christians, of course, assume that 'he is not here' means precisely the opposite: that a personalized Christ-figure is constantly to be encountered (even if in a way that cannot be verified) by the believer. Yet it is possible in Christian teaching, as Panikkar shows, for the absence of God to be interpreted in a positive way. The concept of God as process and as love may enable people to find meaning in what is otherwise a bankrupt currency. And to grasp this understanding of God, people not only have to relinquish some cherished ways of thinking and speaking, they also have to be willing to let go of their *own* self: 'Whoever wants to save his life will lose it.' There is a direct correlation between intellectual and spiritual journeys. Panikkar quotes Gregory of Nyssa to the effect that the spiritual quest is an endless seeking of God: 'Contemplation of God's face consists in journeying toward God ceaselessly, in moving forward constantly in the endless following of the Word.'[7]

The 'wisdom' traditions of India seek to unite a knowledge, of texts and ideas, with practices of meditation and reflection. They are not seen as having to do only with acquiring knowledge, but also with providing stimulus for continuing a spiritual journey. The fact that a fourth-century theologian also regarded the delights and difficulties of the apophatic traditions as providing help in 'moving forward constantly' will provide encouragement to those in today's world who want to move on to more adventurous and helpful concepts of the divine.

The difficulty for the person who wishes to pursue a Christian path of knowledge and understanding – a Christian *jnana* – is in finding places where that might be done. Given the politics of congregational life, it is unlikely that a Christian *jnana* will find a worshipping congregation that is entirely congenial. And if theology is being re-thought, then worship will also need to be reconstructed. It may be that will prove to be possible only by a limiting of words and a much greater use of silence. Quaker meetings are interesting examples of silent worship in which the beliefs of those present remain largely hidden, although the demands made upon the personal resources of the worshippers are much greater than in most other forms of worship. To meditate in silence for the best part of an hour is a demanding activity. Many Christians will prefer places of worship where there is liturgy and music and movement. And that may require compromise, and an acceptance that in public worship not all that is said and done can be subjected to rigorous scrutiny. Curiously, perhaps, ritual and familiar liturgies can provide a more suitable framework for worship than a 'modern' style in which the language of worship and songs, precisely because of its supposed relevance, becomes an obstacle for the thoughtful worshipper.

But it is unlikely that the worship of more than a very few congregations will of itself be able to provide what is needed by the critical and enquiring Christian. Her needs are more likely to be met by a small group of like-minded people, meeting once a month or so for study and reflection, perhaps also for periods of quiet and meditation, and certainly for mutual support. Paradoxically, it may be in a kind of house group that the antidote to house churches may be discovered. There are larger networks, and the SCM Press Trust[8] is only one among many which produce an occasional newsletter, but clearly there is a need for groups of like-minded people – would they necessarily have to be comprised only of Christians? – in local areas to afford regular contact and support. Are churches themselves open enough to recognize such needs, and perhaps to facilitate contact between people who would benefit from mutual support on journeys into uncharted waters?

The idea of a journey is essential to what such groups of people would be doing. They must expect to make progress, and to discover spiritual paths which lead to new ideas, the refreshment of old concepts, and the shaping of practice. In doing this, the practice of a spirituality – of prayer, meditation, and reflection – in some of the ways suggested in chapter 2 is likely to be important for many, but not for all. One of the obvious problems about meditation and quiet reflection is that they are very difficult to do without appropriate time and space. Ideally, days might begin and end with some carefully focused thought, but that will not be easy for the parent harassed by the demands of small children or the man or woman with a demanding job. At best, there may be only one or two occasions during the week when it is possible to slide into a pool of quiet to reflect, not on daily demands, but on underlying purposes and meanings. And for those living in crowded houses, sharing a room and with no space to retreat to, it may only be by going for a walk that any kind of solitude can be found. Certainly, in many homes the demand for even a short period of quiet could only be met by turning off the television!

But most of us can manage to be quiet for some small part of the day. Then it is that we can try to be reasonably systematic about a programme of reflection and meditation. Some ways of doing that have been suggested in chapter 2. In addition to prayer, there will be other ways of feeding the spirit. Short readings often help to focus the mind. For some, it may be helpful to read the Bible, although for others the obscurity of much of the text, and its tendency to throw the mind into paroxysms of criticism and argument, will be more hindrance than help. There are other things to read. What religion at its best is after is also expressed – often better expressed – not in churchy activities but in literature, and art, and music, and poetry.

The second path to spiritual progress found in all the great religions is commended in the *Gita* under the name of *karma*, or action. In general use, the concept of *karma* has to do with personal and caste-related behaviour which may determine a person's future life, both in their present existence and in rebirth. *Karma* also plays an important part in providing the means of accommodating suffering and bad fortune into a widely understood system. Misfortune or disasters may be attributed to the bad *karma* (the result of inappropriate behaviour) of an individual or a group. As with theories in other religions, *karma* does not so much explain suffering as to suggest that suffering is not entirely inexplicable; in some wider scheme, it has some meaning. In the *Bhagavad Gita*, however, the idea of *karma* is presented as a path of social action. Gandhi seized upon this, and having pronounced the *Gita* his favourite scripture, especially commended the chapters which deal with the path of action.[9] As we have seen,[10] the *Gita*'s teaching about doing one's duty without fear of the consequences or expectation of reward under-pinned Gandhi's programme of non-violent resistance to injustice and tyranny. In that striking modern example, there-fore, *karma* is related to political and social action of the kind discussed in chapter 5.

Christians may feel, with some justification, that the Judaeo-Christian tradition has always given a significant place to the application of ethics to public life. The best of modern Christianity has echoed the sentiments expressed by the prophet Amos, who spurned the ritual performances of pilgrim-feasts and sacred ceremonies and even had the audacity to criticize the music of popular worship:

Spare me the sound of your songs;
I shall not listen to the strumming of your lutes.
Instead, let justice flow on like a river and righteousness like a never-failing torrent.[11]

The great tradition of the Jewish ethical prophets was adopted by Jesus, according to the gospel account in which he accepted for his own ministry the words of Isaiah:

The Spirit of the Lord is upon me because he has anointed me;
he has sent me to announce good news to the poor,
to proclaim release for prisoners
and recovery of sight for the blind;
to let the broken victims go free,
to proclaim the year of the Lord's favour.[12]

The Christian tradition of social and political action is undoubtedly of major importance, in spite of the difficulties of applying ethical thinking to complex modern problems and the inhibitions created by the fear of upsetting members of the congregation or influential public figures. Politicians, especially those of the right, have been quick to suggest that church leaders should stick to their 'proper tasks', which are presumably those of saying prayers and exonerating the consciences of people whose daily lives involve them in messier situations. The criticism makes plain a misunderstanding of Christian, and indeed, other religious teaching. Those who have struggled in inner cities around the world to make some sense of faith and hope and love in situations in which economics and politics appear to have removed all three have been much closer to essential Christian teaching. Concern for overseas development has been a major religious as well as secular theme of the post-war years in Europe and north America, as the emergence of such agencies as Christian Aid and CAFOD testify. And in spite of many mistakes and omissions, there is a considerable level of concern for the issues of race relations, homelessness and peace-making.

Those involved in such struggles reflect a long and honourable Christian tradition. In modern times that has been seen in the work of William Wilberforce and his fellow evangelicals who campaigned to end the slave trade; in the tentative attempts of the nineteenth-century Christian socialists to map out some kind of corresponding reality to the theological concept of the kingdom of God; and by twentieth-century Christians who in various ways attempted to unite faith and practice. Such Christian leaders as William Temple (Archbishop of York, 1929–42 and of Canterbury, 1942–44) and George Bell (Bishop of Chichester, 1929–1958) worked valiantly to provide a lead in Christian thinking about social issues and war. Temple played a formative part in the Workers Educational Association, presided over the Conference on Christian Politics, Economics and Citizenship (COPEC) in 1924, and in his book *Christianity and the Social Order* (1942) provided a set of clear aims for Christians to pursue in education and economic affairs. Bell also had the courage to speak out publicly against the policy of the deliberate bombing of German cities during the Second World War. Some of his thinking is reflected in his *Christianity and World Order* (1940).

Since 1945 perhaps the major development in Christian social and political thinking has been concerned with connections between Christian faith and the poor and deprived of the world, and that has led to the development of a number of theologies of liberation. The most creative thinking in liberation theology has occurred in South America, where historically the gulf between the powerful position of the church and the condition of the poor was strikingly obvious. Catholic priests and theologians have turned increasingly to the Bible to locate the roots of a theology related directly to a struggle for peace and justice. The theologians of the movement have often been those involved in political action as well as in the writing of theology. One of the best-known books in this area is *A Theology of Liberation* by Gustavo Gutiérrez, a Peruvian priest who as well as serving as consultant for the Episcopal Conference of Latin America also works among the poor in a Lima slum.[13] The ideas of liberation theology have spread around the world, and have been influential in southern Africa and parts of Asia as well as in Latin America and, indeed, certain areas of Europe and North America. Among the churches in India during the last twenty years there has been a great development of what is called 'Dalit theology', that is, a theology and practice related to the position of converts from low caste or outcaste groups to Christianity. In all of these movements practice and doctrine, the idea of an orthopraxis as well as an orthodoxy, have gone together, so that faith has come to be regarded as being 'verified when informed by love, solidarity, and hunger and thirst for justice'.[14]

The model borrowed from India of the three approaches to a religious life reveals how strong and diverse the Christian intellectual tradition has been, and reminds us how important a way of action has been for Christians. The desire to express faith in social and political action has been much stronger, I suspect, among Christians than among Hindus, in spite of the great examples of Gandhi, Vinoba Bhaave[15] and many others. Those who want to make progress in their religious and spiritual life will want to be involved in at least some of the great issues that have to do with how we treat our brothers and sisters, of all cultures, creeds, and nations. That will mean focusing attention upon development issues, race relations, homelessness, peace-making, justice, and social relationships in which there is equal regard for all. Following the path will involve some level of concern with all these things and more; but in practical concerns, each person will have to order their priorities, and consider what they can do. Just as there needs to be a programme for reflection and meditation, so also there must be a programme for social action. Prayer cannot be a substitute for action, as people may believe when they say, 'well, we cannot actually be involved, but we shall pray for those who are'; but it can be a means of focusing the mind on what needs to be done. Intercession, which is a problem for many people who wonder what it is they expect to happen as the result of their prayers, or how the prayers of a congregation in one part of the world might affect those suffering from disaster in another, can become more relevant. The notion of intercession as something that 'visualizes an alternative future', or of intercessors as those 'who believe the future into being' might refresh a tired concept and give new meaning to praying for others.[16]

The third path in this model is that of *bhakti*, which in Indian terms means loving devotion and fervent worship. Undoubtedly, it is *bhakti*, in one form or another, that underlies most popular religion, in whatever cultural or religious context that may be found. Exuberant worship, ecstatic dance, noisy processions, prayers to God or the gods for healing, the singing of simple devotional songs, are common to popular religion among Christians, Hindus and Buddhists alike. Apart from the use of the name by which God is invoked, there may seem to the detached observer to be remarkably little difference between examples of this kind of religion found in the various great faith systems. With Vivekananda, the adventurous Christian trying to press on with the journey may look back and bless the preceding steps; but he or she will not want to retrace them. Helpful for many, the noise and jollity of the Christian *bhakta* may be unhelpful for others. Too churchy a religion can be very off-putting; one can only stand so much banality. Although worship may need to be constructed in a way that makes connections with surrounding popular cultures, the result will not be suitable for everyone. Others of us will need more silence; more opportunity for worship and fewer words thrown at us. We covet a quiet and peaceful setting for worship, preferably in a place endued with an atmosphere of tranquillity and peace. If worship is to be embellished, we should like it to be by good music, art and literature. Devotion is not only brought to life by merry-making; joy can be created by gentler arts.

The paradigm of three paths may be provide a helpful way of charting the right course on our journey of faith. The three can complement one another, although our background, education, cultural values and psychological make-up may determine that one is more helpful than the others. And whichever path is more naturally ours, we should keep alert to the possibility of progress, which might mean moving on from one path to another. But all are legitimate, and all deserve tolerance from those whose way is different.

Tolerance is a great necessity for those who profess religious faith in the modern world. Strong convictions and the firm adherence to any kind of ideology provide those who hold them with a double-edged weapon. Such people know where they stand, but they may find it difficult to appreciate the fact that others do not share their convictions and yet may have valid insights and important values of their own. To be tolerant of people of other faiths is essential to community relations, and may also bring the benefit of enriching one's own faith. But in a world of much religious intolerance, judgments have to be made and some things excluded. The believer who wishes to practise tolerance and sympathetic understanding may find herself at a disadvantage here. If a fellow believer is intolerant of neighbours of other faiths, is his or her intolerance to be tolerated? If somebody embraces a narrow and exclusive belief which is based on credulity and superstition, are we to regard that as acceptable? The answer, surely, must be 'no'. And if religion is being used to support violence, racial intolerance, or contempt for other people, then we have to criticize and argue with that kind of religion. Religion, we have already noticed, can be a power for good or the cause of great evil. Wars, bigotry, and narrow-minded exclusivity have all been supported by religious beliefs. On the other hand, there are plenty of examples of people who have been stimulated by their religious convictions to campaign for peace, open their hearts and homes to others, and acknowledge the good in people of all faiths and none. Yet there are some expressions of Christianity about which one has to say, 'In the name of Christian faith, I must struggle against that kind of Christianity.' When Christian religion is used – as it has been in Ireland, Serbia and many other places – as an excuse for murder and intolerance of a most extreme kind, then other Christians must say, 'In the name of Christian faith, I must struggle against that kind of Christianity.' The touchstone of such judgments will be the presence or absence of those signs of the love and grace of God so powerfully expressed in the life of Jesus of Nazareth.

Adherents of other religions will recognize the need to take similar stands against extremists in their own traditions, although the criteria for doing so will be different. Hindus in India, appalled by the hijacking of their normally tolerant faith by nationalist politicians of the BJP and the RSS,[17] and by those in Ayodhya and elsewhere who have used the majority status of Hindus in India as an excuse for rabid religious nationalism, will find themselves impelled to say, 'In the name of Hindu religion, I must oppose that kind of Hinduism.' Muslims, too, will find among their co-religionists some who show none of the hospitality to other faiths that the *Qur'an* enjoins for 'people of the Book', and in the face of extreme religious fanaticism will say, 'In the name of Islam, I must oppose that kind of Muslim.'

It is time to campaign against arrogance and exclusivity in religion, and to assert the positive values of tolerance, humility, and the acceptance of those whose religious orientation is different from our own. This is not to commend a naive acceptance of absolutely anything, but to applaud a generosity of mind and spirit which reflects the best of all the great religious traditions.[18] Religions need people who can be confident about not knowing all the answers, and who are capable of asking, with Vincent Donovan:

> . . . what of those who cast aside their arrogance toward other human beings and cultures and religions and are gentle and humble enough to be open to conversion? Are they not the ones 'who shall inherit the earth'?[19]

Conversion can and does happen. People do find themselves enthralled and changed by religious faith, and that often in a healthy, open and accepting fashion. But even for Christians schooled by texts and tradition to regard conversion as a once-for-all turning around to re-orientate their lives (the *metanoia* of the New Testament), there can be an awareness of subsequent conversions and further moments of revelation. As we follow the path we find new levels of understanding and, if we are fortunate, occasional moments of enlightenment as our religious faith fits together with and lights up our experience of the secular world. In that exhilarating and demanding process, faiths other than our own may shed fresh light on what we have received and help us to refine our own faith in the reflection of what we learn from others.

The journey of faith may not after all provide the security we long for but are not granted in our complex, changing, bewildering world. It may do much more for us than that. As we make progress in our religious quest, we may find ourselves, to our surprise, exploring new scenery, crossing cultural boundaries, and as a result waking up to new ways of believing and practising our faith.

Notes

Where publication details are not given, these will be found in the Bibliography which follows these Notes.

1. Written in Pencil on the Flyleaf

1. Letter from The Rt Revd Dr Lesslie Newbigin to the author, 6 April 1967.
2. Letter to the Hebrews 11.1.
3. 'We are practising right speech when we use conversation as a means of coming to know people, to understand them and ourselves. This . . . may seem a little ridiculous if looked at superficially: what else, one might ask, could conversation be used for? Yet one has only to sit in a bus or train and listen to the 'conversations' going on around to realize that they are very rarely examples of right speech. Most so-called conversations are a series of interrupted monologues: each member of the group speaks more or less in order, but no one listens or makes any attempt to respond.' H. Saddhatissa, *The Buddha's Way*, p. 49.
4. William Johnston, *Letters to Contemplatives*, pp. 24–5.
5. *advaita* – the word means 'non-dual', and is used to describe a major school of Indian philosophy. *Advaita* teaches that our knowledge of the phenomenal world is full of contradictions, and that only the absolute, or *Brahman*, is wholly real. *Visishtadvaita* – a philosophy of 'modified non-dualism' which arose out of criticisms of *advaita* made by Ramanuja. It accommodates belief in a God who is to the world as the soul is to the body.
6. Peter D. Bishop, 'Towards a Christian Yoga', *The Expository*

Times Vol. LXXXVII No. 12, September 1976.

7. Peter D. Bishop, *Sermons from St John's.*
8. Bede Griffiths continued to make his home at Kulittalai until his death at the age of 87 in May 1994.
9. *The Raja Yoga of Vivekananda and the Integral Yoga of Aurobindo*, unpublished PhD thesis, University of London, 1973.
10. That this was not the whole story, and that many nineteenth-century missionaries did attempt to understand Hindu culture and religion at considerable depth can be seen from a reading of Kenneth Cracknell, *Justice, Courtesy and Love. Theologians and Missionaries Encountering World Religions, 1846–1914.*
11. Letter from Dom Bede Griffiths to the author, 10 August 1972.
12. DMK – the Dravida Munnetra Kazhagam (Party for the uplift of the Tamils) – came to power as the State Government in 1967, and in one form or another has retained control of Tamilnadu (formerly Madras State) for most of the time since then.
13. Peter D. Bishop, *A Technique for Loving. Non-Violence in Indian and Christian Traditions.*
14. Changes in Higher Education in 1992 included the opportunity for Polytechnics to adopt the name 'university', and so present more accurately what they had long been doing. In September 1992 Brighton Polytechnic became the University of Brighton.
15. Cleo McNelly Kearns, *T.S. Eliot and Indic Traditions. A Study in Poetry and Belief*, p. xiii.

2. Petitioners and Yogis

1. Matthew 7.7; Luke 11.9.
2. The *bodhisattva* is a focus of attention and devotion, especially in Mahayana Buddhism, as an enlightened being who postpones his own entry into *nibbana* in order to help others along the path. Prayers for help in achieving enlightenment may be addressed to the *bodhisattva*. In Hinduism some gurus have come to be worshipped as incarnations, or *avataras*, with supernatural powers of their own.
3. For an analysis of Quaker worship and beliefs associated with it, see Pink Dandelion, *A Sociological Analysis of the Theology*

of Quakers: The Silent Revolution.

4. Gerald Heard, 'Vedanta as the Scientific Approach to Religion', in C. Isherwood (ed.), *Vedanta for the Western World*, p. 55.

5. William Johnston, 'Christian Zen', in *Lord Teach us to Pray*, p. 37.

6. The *Bhagavad Gita*, 6.11,12. Translations of the *Gita* into English vary greatly in quality. Some paraphrase rather than translate the Sanskrit, and in the process produce tendentious versions of the original. Among the best available are R.C. Zaehner, *The Bhagavad Gita. With a Commentary based on the original sources*, and W. J. Johnson, *The Bhagavad Gita. A new translation*. Translations of the *Gita* in this book are my own.

7. Bede Griffiths, *River of Compassion. A Christian Commentary on the Bhagavad Gita*, p. 114.

8. The *Bhagavad Gita*, 5.29.

9. Horst Georg Pöhlmann, *Encounters with Hinduism*, p. 39. Pöhlmann also argues that belief in incarnation and *avataras* brings Christian faith closer to Hinduism than it is to Judaism or Islam.

10. Bede Griffiths, op. cit., pp. 101, 102.

11. James H. Woods, *The Yoga-System of Patanjali*, pp. xvii–xix, concludes that the most substantial part of the Sutras was written between 300 and 500 CE. Heinrich Zimmer suggests that 'the first three books of his [Patanjali's] basic treatise may belong to the second century B.C.' – *Philosophies of India*, p. 282, a period also accepted by S. Radhakrishnan and C.A. Moore, *A Sourcebook in Indian Philosophy*, p. 453. The origins of Yoga itself are much older, possibly going back into the period of the Indus civilization.

12. See Peter D. Bishop, 'Towards a Christian Yoga'.

13. *Hatha* – force, violence, obstinacy. In Yoga, for the practices which have to do especially with the control of the body.

14. See footnote 20, p.141.

15. *Satya*, as Gandhi was fond of reminding people, is derived from *sat*, being, or 'to be'. So, taught Gandhi, truthfulness is that which has true existence and thus must prevail over falsehood, which has the quality of non-existence.

16. Leviticus 19.18; Matthew 19.19, 22.39; Mark 12.31; Luke

10.27.
17. Matthew 6.19. But see the whole of 6.19–34.
18. Horst Georg Pöhlmann, op. cit., p. 70.
19. See, for example, Evelyn Underhill, *Mysticism*, pp. 198–9.
20. Quoted in William Johnston, *Lord Teach us to Pray*, pp. 8–9.
21. Although incorporated into Christian liturgies, this famous prayer is found first in the Brihadaranyaka Upanishad, 1:iii:28.
22. See also Peter D. Bishop, *Clinging to Faith*, ch. 20, and *The Christian and People of Other Faiths*, ch. 8.
23. Graham Smith, *Prayer Words*, pp. 35ff.
24. *Pratyaharana* – bringing back; withholding; withdrawing from. *Pratyhara* – the retreat of troops; withholding the senses from external objects.
25. Sunnyu Suzuki, *Zen Mind, Beginner's Mind*, quoted William Johnston, 'Christian Zen', in *Lord Teach us to Pray*, p 116.
26. In a book on Christian prayer, Hubert Northcott wrote: 'When our prayer begins, stillness must be its keynote, stillness of body as well as of mind. We must hold ourselves quietly before God, allow His presence and His peace to surround us.' *The Venture of Prayer*, p. 177.
27. *Dharana*, concentration, comes from a root which means to grasp, or to be attached – *dha*.
28. Galatians 5.22, 23.
29. I.K. Taimni, *The Science of Yoga*, pp. 206–7.
30. *The Dark Night of the Soul*, Book II, Ch. 18, para.5, quoted Northcott, op. cit., p. 177.
31. Evelyn Underhill, op. cit., p. 317.
32. Ben Okri, *Birds of Heaven*, pp. 13–14.
33. Revelation 8.1.
34. Luke 4.18,19. See Isaiah 61.1–3.
35. Matthew, Mark and Luke.
36. William Johnston wrote of Jesus: '. . .one of his great mystical experiences takes place at the time of his baptism . . . Mark observes that *Jesus saw*. It was the inner eye, the eye of love that saw; and Jesus realized in the Spirit that he was the Son of the Father.' *The Inner Eye of Love. Mysticism and Religion*, p. 50.
37. Rowan Williams, in Gordon Wakefield (ed.), *A Dictionary of Christian Spirituality*, pp. 109–10.

38. See Mark 1.35; Luke 3.21, 4.42, 5.16, 6.12, 9.18, 9.28, 11.1, 22.41.
39. For St Teresa and St John of the Cross, see Colin P. Thompson in Wakefield (ed.), op. cit., p. 232.
40. This is part of the 'Four Applications of Mindfulness', which include continually observing the body in the light of the instruction of the Buddha: 'Moreover, bhikkhu, when one is walking, one is aware of it: "I am walking". Similarly, when one is standing or sitting down, one is aware of one's posture.' Trevor Ling, *The Buddha's Philosophy of Man. Early Indian Buddhist Dialogues*, p. 176.
41. John F. Wickham, 'Ignatian Contemplation Today', in Philip Sheldrake (ed.), *The Way of Ignatius Loyola. Contemporary Approaches to the Spiritual Exercises*, p. 145.
42. Raimundo Panikkar, *The Silence of God. The Answer of the Buddha*, p. 155.

3. Atheists, Agnostics, and Believers

1. Peter Brierley, *Christian England. What the English Church Census Reveals*, gives a figure of 27% for those who declared themselves to be atheists or agnostics. See also Peter D. Bishop, *Clinging to Faith*, pp. 31–6.
2. Matthew 5.45.
3. See the reference to Horst Georg Pöhlmann and his description of Hindu belief as 'pluralistic monotheism', p. 33.
4. A number often used of Hindu gods, reflecting the apparently limitless range of concepts of God. In the *Brihadaranyaka Upanishad*, III, ix,1–9, the sage Yajnavalkya is asked how many gods there are. His initial answer is 'As many as are mentioned in the invocatory formula in the hymn to the All-gods – three hundred and three and three thousand and three'. Pressed further – 'how many gods are there really' – he reduces this number to thirty-three, then six, three, two and finally One. His questioner then asks: 'Yes, but which are those three hundred and three and those three thousand and three?' Yajnavalkya answers: 'These are only their attributes . . .' And after further discussion and enumeration, answers the question: 'Which is the one God?' by saying: 'The breath of life, and that

is *Brahman*, the beyond.' *Hindu Scriptures*, translated by R. C. Zaehner.

5. The *Vedas* are the earliest sacred writings of the Hindus, and are regarded as the revealed texts of orthodox Hinduism. Written in Sanskrit, they are made up of a collection of hymns attributed to what most scholars consider to have been the early Indo-European conquerors of northern India: the *Rig Veda*, hymns to the gods; the *Soma Veda*, verses for chanting at sacrifices; the *Yajur Veda*, instructions about sacrifice; and the *Atharva Veda*, a collection of charms and spells used for curing diseases. The later writings of the *Brahmanas*, the *Aranyakas*, and finally the *Upanishads*, were added to the early writings, and together they constitute the Vedic literature.

6. Raimundo Panikkar, op. cit., p. 205.

7. Most of the *Upanishads* are believed to have been written between 800 and 300 BCE. The conventional date of birth of Siddhartha Buddha is 563 BCE, although some scholars now suggest a later date, perhaps as late as 500 BCE.

8. In a four-fold classification of society Hindus have been divided into *brahmins*, priests and scholars, *kshatriyas*, warriors and rulers, *vaisya*, merchants, and *sudra*, labourers. This *varna* system is not the same as caste (*jati*), although caste groups are located within the *varna* categories. The more purist English rendering of the highest group is *brahman*; here I have used *brahmin* to avoid confusion with *Brahman*, ultimate reality, and to approximate more closely to the common pronounciation.

9. Raimundo Panikkar, op. cit., p. 92.

10. The Nicene creed in its earliest form at the Council of Nicaea in 325 CE, and in its longer form confirmed at the Council of Constantinople in 381. The Apostles' Creed was known by that name from around 390, but evolved from the shorter Roman creed that had been in use since at least the end of the second century.

11. For a vigorous exposition of this position, see S. Radhakrishnan, *Eastern Religions and Western Thought*, especially chapter VII, in which he wrote: 'The strife between Arius and Athanasius still continues in the hearts of men. Athanasius weaned the Church from her traditions of tolerance and

scholarship, of Clement and Origen. Nicene orthodoxy gained victory over Hellenistic and heretical systems.'

12. See Richard Gombrich and Gananath Obeyesekere, *Buddhism Transformed. Religious Change in Sri Lanka.*

13. In *A Vision to Pursue*, Keith Ward drew attention to the route to Aquinas that leads from Aristotle via the Muslim al-Ghazali and the Jewish scholar Maimonides. p. 168.

14. Paul Tillich, *Systematic Theology*, Vol. 1, p. 181.

15. 'If God is no longer "cause" there is no longer any need to seek to "prove" God. Only a "cause" can be searched for, only a "cause" has need of "proofs" and "demonstrations".' Raimundo Panikkar, op. cit., p. 205, fn.74.

16. A. Falaturi, 'How can a Muslim experience God given Islam's radical monotheism?', in A. Schimmell & A. Falaturi (eds), *We Believe in One God*, p. 78.

17. Paul Tillich, op. cit., p. 234.

18. The tradition of the Scholastics may be said to have begun with Augustine; it especially includes many of the great mediaeval theologians – John Scotus Erigena, Anselm, Abelard and Thomas Aquinas.

19. Paul Tillich, op. cit., p. 227.

20. Tillich wrote: 'Thus it follows that everything religion has to say about God, including his qualities, actions and manifestations, has a symbolic character – the meaning of "God" is completely missed if one takes the symbolic language literally.' *Systematic Theology*, Vol. 2, p. 10.

21. Swami Vivekananda, *The Complete Works*, Vol.3, pp. 423–4.

22. II Cor. 4.4.

23. 'The very concept of the Trinity is, in a way, an attempt to express the same intuition – namely, that what is, what one can contact, what can be uttered, as it were, is the Logos, and not the Father,' Raimundo Panikkar, op. cit., p. 166.

24. John 1.18.

25. William Temple once wrote, 'He [Jesus] does not reveal all that is meant by the word God. There ever remains the unsearchable abyss of Deity. But he reveals what it vitally concerns us to know. He reveals God as Father.' *Readings in St John's Gospel*, p. 18.

26. William Johnston, 'Christian Zen', op. cit., pp. 40–1.

27. A hymn by Reginald Heber, written in 1819 and probably first published in 1823, the year Heber left England to become Bishop of Calcutta. There are indications that his Indian experience modified his crude earlier views. See Derrick Hughes, *Bishop Sahib. A Life of Reginald Heber*.

28. See Roger Hooker, *What is Idolatry?*, pp. 7–9, and *Themes in Hinduism and Christianity. A Comparative Study*, p. 233.

29. Chandogya Upanishad, III, xiii, 7. Translated by R.C. Zaehner, op. cit.

30. Ibid, VI,xi,3.

31. See G. W. H. Lampe, *God as Spirit*. 'It is to express the concept of immanent creative activity of the transcendent Creator that we use the term "Spirit", referring to the one God, transcendent and immanent, as he makes himself known to us in his outgoings towards us which is also his indwelling within us.' pp. 207–8.

32. 'Consciousness of community . . . is always associated with the Spirit – it was the communal experience of enthusiastic worship of *koinonia*, participation in the one Spirit, that made the first disciples a community, a distinct sect, a church.' James D. G. Dunn, *Jesus and the Spirit*, p. 145.

33. John V. Taylor, *The Go-Between God*, p. 17.

34. Translation of the final lines of *The Divine Comedy* by Dorothy Sayers in her introduction to *Hell*, Penguin, 1949, Vol.1, p. 9, quoted Taylor, ibid, p. 46. See also Bishop, *Clinging to Faith*, pp. 40–1.

35. 1 John 4.7–8, 12,16.

36. 'A modern formulation – with ancient and Christian roots – approaches the problem of the Being and Nonbeing of God within the notion of God as Love. Through the subtle exegesis of a . . . text (translating 1 Cor. 13.2 as 'without love, I am not, I do not exist') it is concluded that being is Love. We must proceed in this direction . . . in full cognizance that God is Love precisely because God is not being; God is love, and love is neither being nor is being love . . .' Raimundo Panikkar, op. cit., pp. 130–1.

37. Marcus Braybrooke, *A Time to Meet*, p. 7.

38. In process theology it is 'impossible to think of God except as intimately related to everything that is capable in some sense of

experiencing, responding to and suffering with what goes on in the world. Consequently, the concept appears to some to be more consistent with the God of the Christian gospel than the immutable, impassible static associations of the classical concept.' N.H.G. Robinson and D.W.D. Shaw in Richardson and Bowden (eds), *A New Dictionary of Christian Theology*, pp. 241–2.

4. *The Cause or Cure of Selfishness*

1. Don Cupitt, *Taking Leave of God*, p. 101.
2. John Robinson, *Honest to God*, p. 82.
3. Psalm 90.
4. Translated from the Spanish by Colin Thompson. See the reflection on Teresa's poem in Chapter 1 of Bishop, *Clinging to Faith*, pp. 3–10.
5. The constituents (*khandha*) of the self are: the physical and material form (*rupa*); sense-perception (*vedana*); consciousness (*sana*); intellectual faculties (*sankhara*); and discrimination (*vinnana*).
6. Steven Collins, *Selfless Persons. Imagery and Thought in Therevada Buddhism*.
7. Ibid, p. 183.
8. Ibid, p. 119.
9. 'According to the teaching of the Buddha, the idea of self is an imaginary, false belief which has no corresponding reality, and it produces harmful thoughts of "me" and "mine", selfish desire, craving, impurities and problems. It is the source of all the troubles of the world from personal conflicts to wars between nations. In short, to this false view can be traced all the evil in the world.' W. Rahula, *What the Buddha Taught*, quoted Collins, op. cit., p. 4.
10. Mark 8.34.
11. William Johnston, *Letters to Contemplatives*, p. 68.
12. See the comments on The *Bhagavad Gita*, pp. 31.
13. Bede Griffiths, *River of Compassion*, op. cit., p. 31.
14. M. K. Gandhi, *An Autobiography*, Vol.1 of S. Narayan (ed.), *The Selected Works of Mahatma Gandhi*, p. 101.
14. Juan Mascaro, *The Bhagavad Gita*. Swami Chidbavananda,

The Bhagavad Gita. This also includes the Sanskrit text and a commentary.

16. Mark 8.34.

17. An interesting difference between the Gospels is that Mark and Luke present the teaching as though it were given to a crowd of people (Mark: *ton ochlon*; Luke: *pros pantas*), including the disciples, while Matthew presents it as having been given only to the disciples (*eipen tois mathetais autou*) perhaps as part of his emphasis on the training of the twelve for their future role as teachers and leaders of the church.

18. See Vincent Taylor, *The Gospel According to St Mark*, p. 380; D. E. Nineham, *Saint Mark*, pp. 223–32; and Morna D. Hooker, *The Gospel According to St Mark*, pp. 204–13.

19. Morna Hooker, op. cit., p. 208.

20. Four of the traditional five precepts are shared with Jainism and Hinduism: non-violence (*ahimsa*); not stealing (*asteya*); celibacy (*brahmacarya*); truthfulness (*satya*) – in Buddhism, avoiding 'false speech'. The fifth precept of Hinduism and Jainism – not coveting (*aparigraha*) – is so central to Buddhist teaching as a whole that is not included as a precept; instead, Buddhism includes a rule about not using drugs or alcohol, aimed at maintaining mental clarity.

21. Peggy Morgan, 'Orthodoxy and Openness: the Experience of Buddhist Children', in Brian Gates (ed.), *Freedom and Authority in Religions and Religious Education*, p. 121.

5. *Causes of Conflict or Paths to Peace?*

1. Derek Worlock and David Sheppard, *Better Together*, p. 290.

2. A fascinating account of how the history of religions fought off attempts to incorporate its work into, successively, departments of theology and of Marxist studies in the University of Leipzig is given in Kurt Rudolph, *Historical Fundamentals and the Study of Religions*.

3. John Bowker, 'World Religions: the Boundaries of Belief and Unbelief' in Brian Gates (ed.), op. cit., p. 3.

4. See Peter D. Bishop, 'Victorian Values? Some antecedents of a religiously plural society', in R. Hooker and N. Sargant (eds),

Belonging to Britain: Christian Perspectives on Religion and Identity in a Plural Society.

5. For a brief account of these communities in Britain, see Part 3 of Peter D. Bishop, *Thinking Things Through. 3. The Christian and People of Other Faiths.* It should be noted that although there are Buddhists from SE Asia in Britain, the majority of British Buddhists are converts from the population at large.

6. The 1988 Education Reform Act stipulated that religious education in schools should 'reflect the fact that religious traditions in Great Britain are in the main Christian whilst taking account of the teaching and practice of the other principal religions represented in Great Britain'. Although many educationalists regard as regressive the implied requirement to focus at least 50% of RE lessons on Christianity, the Act has for the first time made the inclusion of some teaching of other religious faiths compulsory.

7. Georges Khodr, 'Violence and the Gospel', *Cross Currents*, 37 (Winter 1987–88) quoted in Walter Wink, *Engaging the Powers. Discernment and Resistance in a World of Domination*, p. 26.

8. Herbert Butterfield, *Christianity, Diplomacy and War*, p. 38.

9. Gregory Baum and Harold Wells (eds), *The Reconciliation of Peoples. Challenge to the Churches*, p. vii.

10. Peter D. Bishop, *A Technique for Loving. Non-Violence in Indian and Christian Traditions.*

11. M.K. Gandhi, *An Autobiography*, p. 101.

12. Gandhi supported the cause of the Western allies in the First World War, and even acted briefly as a recruiting agent for the Viceroy in a tour of the Punjab in early 1918. With the outbreak of the Second World War Gandhi supported a policy of non-co-operation, culminating in the Quit India Movement in 1942.

13. Wink points to the parallel in Ephesians 6.13: 'take up the whole armour of God, so that you may be able to withstand (literally, draw up ranks in battle) on that evil day . . .' op. cit., p. 185.

14. Ibid, p. 185.

15. Some of this material was worked out in a different context in my chapter on 'War, Peace-Keeping and Terrorism' in Cyril S. Rodd (ed.), *New Occasions Teach New Duties. Christian*

Ethics for Today.

16. Peter Calvocoressi, *A Time for Peace.*

17. The National Christian Council of India, The Christian Institute for the Study of Religion and Society, The Fellowship of Reconciliation (India), *Christians and the Prevention of War in an Atomic Age*, p. 10.

18. As reported in *The Friend*, 21 March 1997.

19. Anguttaranikaya, III.208, quoted by H. Saddhatissa, *Buddhist Ethics*, pp. 87ff.

20. Trevor Ling traced the history of wars in Myanmar and Thailand, and concluded that: 'The historical record of the Buddhist kingdoms of South-East Asia does not support the view that where Buddhist institutions and ideas have a prominent place in national life the consequences will be peaceful international relations. Nor is there any clear evidence that in countries where Buddhism is the State religion national wars have been regarded as un-Buddhist activities. The evidence suggests, on the contrary, that Buddhism in South-East Asia has been successfully employed to reinforce the policies and interests of national rulers, often in their competition with one another for resources or prestige.' *Buddhism, Imperialism and War*, p. 136.

21. Arend Th. van Leeuwen, *Christianity in World History*, p. 401.

22. From *The Alternative Service Book*, Hodder and Stoughton, 1980.

23. An indigenous British Church was represented by bishops at the Council of Arles in 314. The first recorded British martyr, St Alban, was thought to have died in the Diocletian persecution of 305, but one manuscript claims that he suffered his martyrdom much earlier, in the time of Septimius Severus, around 209. And an original theologian, Pelagius, travelled from Britain in the late fourth century to teach in Rome.

24. Quoted by Esther De Waal in *A World Made Whole. Rediscovering the Celtic Tradition*, pp. 61–2.

25. Rabindranath Tagore, *Tapovana*, quoted V. Shiva, *Staying Alive: Women, Ecology and Development*, p. 55.

26. Ian Harris, 'Buddhism' in Jean Holm and John Bowker (eds), *Attitudes to Nature*, p. 9.

27. Ibid, p. 11.

28. S. Batchelor, *Education in a Plural Society: A Buddhist Perspective*, World Council of Churches Interlink Project, Geneva, 1989, quoted by Peggy Morgan in Brian Gates, op. cit., p. 125.

29. *Yajur Veda*, V 36:17; *Atharva Veda*, XIX 9:94, quoted Anuradha Roman Choudhury, 'Hindus', in Jean Holm and John Bowker, op. cit., pp. 67–8.

6. Following the Path

1. See p. 31.

2. Vivekananda's personal name was Narendra Nath. He was given the name Vivekananda (the bliss of discrimination) shortly before his journey to the USA to speak for Hinduism at the World Parliament of Religions in 1893.

3. For a brief and accessible description of *advaita*, see Gavin Flood, *An Introduction to Hinduism*, pp. 239–42. See also pp. 58–9 above.

4. *The Complete Works of Swami Vivekananda*, Vol. 3, p. 422. See also pp .58–9 above.

5. See pp. 52–4 above.

6. Raimundo Panikkar, op. cit., p. 131.

7. Gregory of Nyssa, *De Vita Moysis*, PG 44:941, in Panikkar, op. cit., p. 144.

8. The registered office of SCM Press Trust is The Diocese of Birmingham, Church House, 175 Harborne Park Road, Birmingham B17 0BQ.

9. 'I have endeavoured to show that its (the *Gita*'s) message consists in the performance of one's duty with detachment. The theme of the *Gita* is contained in the Second Chapter, and the way to carry out the message is found in the Third Chapter (which deals with *karma*).' M. K. Gandhi, in *Harijan*, Dec. 16, 1939, and quoted in M. K. Gandhi, *Gita – My Mother*, p. 15.

10. Above, pp. 80–1.

11. Amos 5.23–4.

12. Luke 4.18,19: Isaiah 61.1–2.

13. Gustavo Gutiérrez, *A Theology of Liberation*.

14. Dan Cohn Sherbok, 'Liberation Theology', in *A New Dictionary of Christian Theology*, p. 396.

15. Vinoba Bhaave, born in Maharashtra in 1895, was a follower

of Gandhi and after Independence a vigorous campaigner for
land reform, personally demanding that large landlords should
hand over part of their land to the peasants.

16. The phrases are from Walter Wink, op. cit., pp. 298 and 304.
17. The Bharatiya Janata Party and the Rashtriya Swayamsevak
    Sangh.
18. See Peter D. Bishop, *Clinging to Faith*, p. 153.
19. Vincent Donovan, *The Church in the Midst of Creation*, p.

Bibliography

Baum, G. and Wells, H. (eds.), *The Reconciliation of Peoples. Challenge to the Churches*, WCC, Geneva & Orbis, Maryknoll 1997.

Bishop, Peter D., *Sermons from St John's*, CLS/ISPCK, Madras and Delhi 1971.

——, *Words in World Religions*, SCM Press 1979.

——, *A Technique for Loving. Non-Violence in Indian and Christian Traditions*, SCM Press 1981.

——, *Clinging to Faith*, Epworth Press 1996.

——, *Thinking Things Through 3. The Christian and People of Other Faiths*, Epworth Press 1997.

——, and Michael Darton (eds.), *The Encyclopedia of World Faiths*, Macdonald/Orbis 1987 .

Brandon, S. G. F., *The Fall of Jerusalem and the Christian Church*, 2nd edn, London 1957.

——, *Jesus and the Zealots*, Manchester University Press 1967.

Braybrooke, M., *A Time to Meet*, SCM Press 1990.

Brierley, P., *Christian England. What the English Church Census Reveals*, Marc Europe 1991.

Butterfield, H., *Christianity, Diplomacy and War*, Wyvern Books 1962.

Calvocoressi, Peter, *A Time for Peace*, Hutchinson 1987.

Ceadel, Michael, *Pacifism in Britain, 1914–1945*, Clarendon Press 1980.

Chidbavananda, Swami (trans.), *The Bhagavad Gita*, Tapovanam Publishing House, Tirupparaitturai, Tamilnadu 1965.

Coggins, R. J. and Houlden, J. L.(eds.), *A Dictionary of Biblical Interpretation*, SCM Press 1990.

Collins, S., *Selfless Persons. Imagery and Thought in Therevada Buddhism*, CUP 1982.

Cracknell, K., *Justice, Courtesy and Love*, Epworth Press 1995.

Cupitt, D., *Taking Leave of God*, SCM Press 1980.

Dandelion, P., *A Sociological Analysis of the Theology of Quakers. The Silent Revolution*, Edwin Mellen 1996.

de Mello, Anthony, *Sadhana. A Way to God. Christian Exercises in Eastern Form*, Image Books, Doubleday, NY 1984.

De Waal, Esther, *A World Made Whole. Rediscovering the Celtic Tradition*, Fount 1991.

Donovan, Vincent, *The Church in the Midst of Creation*, SCM Press 1989.

Dunn, James D.G., *Jesus and the Spirit*, SCM Press 1975.

Flood, G., *An Introduction to Hinduism*, CUP 1996.

Gandhi, M.K., *An Autobiography* in S. Narayan (ed.), *The Selected Works of Mahatma Gandhi*, Navajivan Publishing House, Ahmedabad, India 1968.

——, *Gita – My Mother* (ed. Anand T. Hingorani), Pearl Publications, Bombay 1965.

Gates, Brian (ed.), *Freedom and Authority in Religions and Religious Education*, Cassell 1996.

Gombrich, R. and Obeyesekere, G., *Buddhism Transformed. Religious Change in Sri Lanka*, Princeton University Press 1988.

Griffiths, Bede, *The Golden String*, Catholic Book Club, London 1954.

——, *Return to the Centre*, Collins 1976.

——, *The Marriage of East and West*, Collins 1982.

——, *River of Compassion. A Christian Commentary on the Bhagavad Gita*, Amity House, Warwick, N.Y. 1987.

Gutiérrez, G., *A Theology of Liberation*, SCM Press 1974.

Holm, J. and Bowker, J. (eds), *Attitudes to Nature*, Pinter Publishers Ltd 1994.

Hooker, Morna D., *The Gospel According to St Mark*, A. & C. Black 1991.

Hooker, R., *Themes in Hinduism and Christianity. A Comparative Study*, Verlag Peter Lang, Frankfurt 1989.

——, *What Is Idolatry?* British Council of Churches, London 1986.

Hooker, R. and Sargant, N., (eds.), *Belonging to Britain: Christian Perspectives on Religion and Identity in a Plural Society*, CCBI, London 1991.

Hughes, Derrick, *Bishop Sahib. A Life of Reginald Heber*, Churchman Publications 1986.

Isherwood, C. (ed.), *Vedanta for the Modern World*, Allen and Unwin 1963.

James, William, *The Varieties of Religious Experience* (1902), Fontana 1962.

Johnson, W. J., *The Bhagavad Gita, A new translation*, OUP (The World's Classics) 1994.

Johnston, W., *Lord Teach us to Pray*, Collins Fount 1990.

——, *The Inner Eye of Love. Mysticism and Religion*, Collins Fount 1981.

——, *Letters to Contemplatives*, HarperCollins Fount 1991.

Kearns, Cleo McNelly, *T. S. Eliot and Indic Traditions. A Study in Poetry and Belief*, CUP 1987.

Lampe, G.W.H., *God as Spirit*, Clarendon Press 1967; reissued SCM Press 1983.

Ling, T. (ed.), *The Buddha's Philosophy of Man. Early Indian Buddhist Dialogues*, J. M. Dent 1981.

Ling, T., *Buddhism, Imperialism and War*, Allen and Unwin 1979.

Mascaro, Juan (trans.), *The Bhagavad Gita*, Penguin 1962.

National Christian Council of India, with CISRS & FOR (India), *Christians and the Prevention of War in an Atomic Age*, Bangalore, India 1960.

Nineham, D.E., *The Gospel of Saint Mark*, Penguin 1969.

Northcott, H., *The Venture of Prayer*, SPCK 1962.

Okri, Ben, *Birds of Heaven*, Phoenix 1996.

Panikkar, R., *The Silence of God. The Answer of the Buddha*, Orbis Books, Maryknoll 1990.

Pohlmann, H.G., *Encounters with Hinduism*, SCM Press 1996.

Radhakrishnan, S., *Eastern Religions and Western Thought*, OUP 1940.

Radhakrishnan, S. & Moore, C.A. (eds), *A Sourcebook in Indian Philosophy*, Princeton University Press 1957.

Richardson, A. and Bowden, J. (eds), *A New Dictionary of Christian Theology*, SCM Press 1983.

Robinson, J., *Honest to God*, SCM Press 1963.

Rodd, C.S. (ed.), *New Occasions Teach New Duties. Christian Ethics for Today*, T. & T. Clark 1995.

Rudolph, Kurt, *Historical Fundamentals and the Study of Religions*, Macmillan, NY 1985.

Saddhatissa, H., *The Buddha's Way*, Allen & Unwin 1975.

——, *Buddhist Ethics*, Allen & Unwin 1976.

Schimmel, A. & Falaturi, A. (eds), *We Believe in One God. The Experience of God in Christianity and Islam*, Burns & Oates 1979.

Sheldrake, Philip (ed.), *The Way of Ignatius Loyola. Contemporary Approaches to the Spiritual Exercises*, SPCK 1991.

Shiva, V., *Staying Alive: Women, Ecology and Development*, Zed Books, 1989.

Sivanandan, Swami, *Yoga Practice*, D.B. Taraporevala Sons & Co., Bombay 1965.

Smith, Graham, *Prayer Words. An Exercise in Meditative Prayer*, Burns and Oates/David Lowell Publishing 1991.

Taimni, I.K., *The Science of Yoga*, Adyar, Madras, 3rd edn, 1968.

Taylor, J.V., *The Go-Between God*, SCM Press 1972.

Taylor, Vincent, *The Gospel According to St Mark*, Macmillan 1959.

Temple, William, *Readings in St John's Gospel*, Macmillan 1947.

Tillich, Paul, *Systematic Theology*, (3 Vols) James Nisbet 1953–64; reissued SCM Press 1978, 1997.

Underhill, Evelyn, *Mysticism*, Methuen (University Paperbacks) 1960 (first published 1911).

van Leeuwen, A.Th., *Christianity in World History*, Edinburgh House Press 1964.

Vivekananda, Swami, *The Complete Works*, (8 Vols) Advaita Ashrama, Calcutta, 11th edn 1962.

Wakefield, Gordon S., (ed.) *A Dictionary of Christian Spirituality*, SCM Press 1983.

Ward, Keith, *A Vision to Pursue*, SCM Press 1991.

Wink, Walter, *Engaging the Powers. Discernment and Resistance in a World of Domination*, Fortress Press, Minneapolis 1992.

Woods, James H., *The Yoga System of Patanjali*, Motilal Banarsidass, Delhi, 3rd edn 1966.

Worlock, D. and Sheppard, D., *Better Together*, Penguin 1989.

Zaehner, R.C. (trans.), *Hindu Scriptures*, J.M. Dent 1966.

——, (trans.) *The Bhagavad Gita. With a Commentary based on the original sources*, Clarendon Press 1969.

Zimmer, H., *Philosophies of India*, Princeton University Press 1989.

Index